ITTED TO

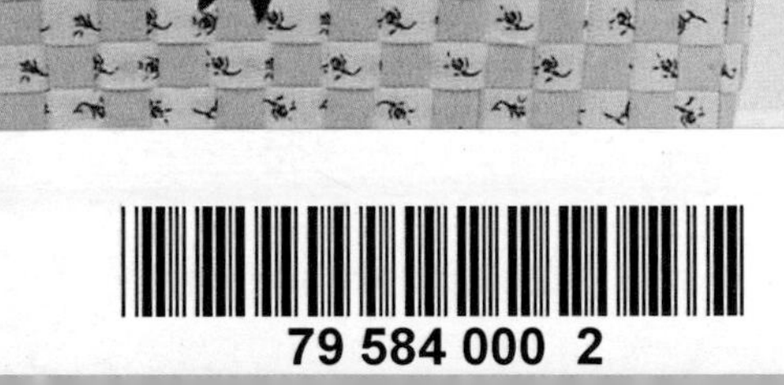

KNITTED TOYS

25 fresh and fabulous designs for tiny tots

Zoë Mellor

hamlyn

This book is dedicated to our great friends Max, Titch, Tilly, Elliott and Flynn with love xx

An Hachette UK Company
www.hachette.co.uk

First published in Great Britain in 2006
by Hamlyn,
a division of Octopus Publishing Group Ltd
Endeavour House
189 Shaftesbury Avenue
London
WC2H 8JY
www.octopusbooks.co.uk

This edition published in 2011

This material was previously published as *Knitted Toys*

ISBN 978-0-600-62381-6

A CIP catalogue record for this book is available from the British Library.

Printed and bound in China

10 9 8 7 6 5 4 3 2 1

Note
Keep all small items used in the projects in this book, such as buttons and sequins, out of reach of young children.

contents

introduction

Knitted toys are so loveable because they evoke a sense of nostalgia and so bring out the child in us all. In this book I have included toys for all ages in a range of styles. There are some classic projects that have been given a modern twist, and some toys that really haven't been knitted before. Classics include the big-foot bunny and the teddy on pages 72 and 64, and one of my favourite retro projects is the owl cushion on page 114.

The stripy ball on page 128 reminds me of one I had when I was young and is a must for any little person. The monkey on page 78 is one of my son's favourites – he especially enjoys folding its long arms and legs. My three-year-old daughter, Kitty, is in love with the dollies and their pretty clothes.

A great thing about knitting toys is that by using a different yarn or colours you can create a new variation on a favourite design, allowing you to knit them over and over again without getting bored by the result. Vary the toy further by finishing it with traditional button eyes for a sweet, old-fashioned look or using felt appliqué features for a more quirky style.

Many of the toys offer a great opportunity to use up small amounts of yarn from your stash of odd balls and leftovers. So go on, experiment, have fun and wow your friends and family with a collection of knitted toys that will make everyone smile.

Happy knitting

Zoë Mellor

yarns

When creating knitted toys, it is important to think about how they feel as well as how they look. It is touch as well as their features that makes them memorable. I always use good-quality yarns to knit with, because I think that if you are going to invest all that effort in knitting something, it should feel gorgeous as well as look great.

Different yarns have different properties and can radically change the style and appearance of what you are knitting. If you knit the same toy in a different yarn, it will change the tension/gauge of your knitting and so the size of the toy will change.

As colour has such a strong effect on design, changing the colours of the toys will also make them look very different. Be sure to take the opportunity to try different colours from those I have used. You'll get a lot of satisfaction knitting up swatches and experimenting with colours that catch your eye. Adding your own touches to the toys will just make them even more special.

choosing yarn

It is a good idea to buy the yarns recommended in the knitting patterns as I have chosen each one carefully to suit that particular toy. The chosen yarn works with the pattern to create the size and style of my design, so by using the specified yarn you will achieve the same toy as is in the book. However, as toys do not actually have to fit in the same way as garments do, you can experiment with yarns and the size of the toy will vary – perhaps your experiments will create great new variations. As so many children have sensitive skin I find it is best to use natural yarns. Here are some of my favourites.

wool This is traditionally associated with knitting. It is springier than cotton, but can be a little itchy for sensitive skins. Its texture can look great, especially on toys like the gingerbread man (see page 68) where it is washed and shrunk to make a felted fabric.

Wool takes dye well and is available in loads of colours. Some wools are softer than others and some are treated so that they are machine-washable, which is a great modern improvement. However, these wools are not ideal for felting. So if you are doing this, choose wool which is hand-wash only, as this will probably felt best.

cotton This natural fibre takes dye well and can be found in lots of colours. It is great for making toys from, but is less springy and fluffy than wool, so when finishing the toy you may have to be very neat in sewing it up. The stitches are more pronounced and it

feels smooth next to your skin. If you maintain a fairly tight tension/gauge, cotton will hold its shape well.

cotton-and-wool-mixed yarn These combine the best of both yarns. Cotton-and-wool mixes are not suitable for felted toys, but are more elastic than pure cotton. They are also fluffier and more forgiving if you don't always have perfect tension when knitting. Cotton and wool mixes are not itchy on the skin and the knitting generally holds its shape very well.

cashmere This is amazingly soft and luxurious to the touch and would make a fabulous keepsake or special toy. Like wool, it holds its shape well and although it is fluffy it is great for children with sensitive skin to cuddle up to.

yarn and dye lots

Yarn is dyed in batches and therefore dye lots can vary greatly. It is always best to check the dye lot number on the label to ensure that the main part of your toy is all in the same shade. For colours dotted around the toy or on stripes, the dye lot won't matter so you can experiment and use up old bits of yarn.

substituting yarn

If you substitute yarn it is best to try and find one of a similar thickness so that the tension/gauge will be similar. If you choose a radically different yarn your toy may look very different and could either be much shorter and stubbier or thinner and more spindly, depending on how chunky or fine the substitute yarn is.

tension/gauge

Tension/gauge is, quite simply, the measurement of the tightness or looseness of the knitted fabric.

On most yarn labels the recommended tension/gauge is given in terms of the number of stitches and the number of rows over 10 cm (4 in) of stocking/stockinette stitch. Tension/gauge determines the size of your knitted pieces so if your stitch and row counts are very different to the ones given, change your needle size to compensate. Everyone knits differently, so you must do this for the best results.

Generally, the finer the yarn, the smaller the needle size and the thicker the yarn, the bigger the needle size. Many of the toys in this book are in medium-weight yarn and so you will see your knits grow quite quickly – which is always satisfying.

Once you have decided on a toy to make, it is important to check your tension/gauge by knitting a swatch before you leap into your project. I know many knitters get too excited at the thought of starting their project and they don't bother with this important step. But please do knit a tension/gauge swatch – it

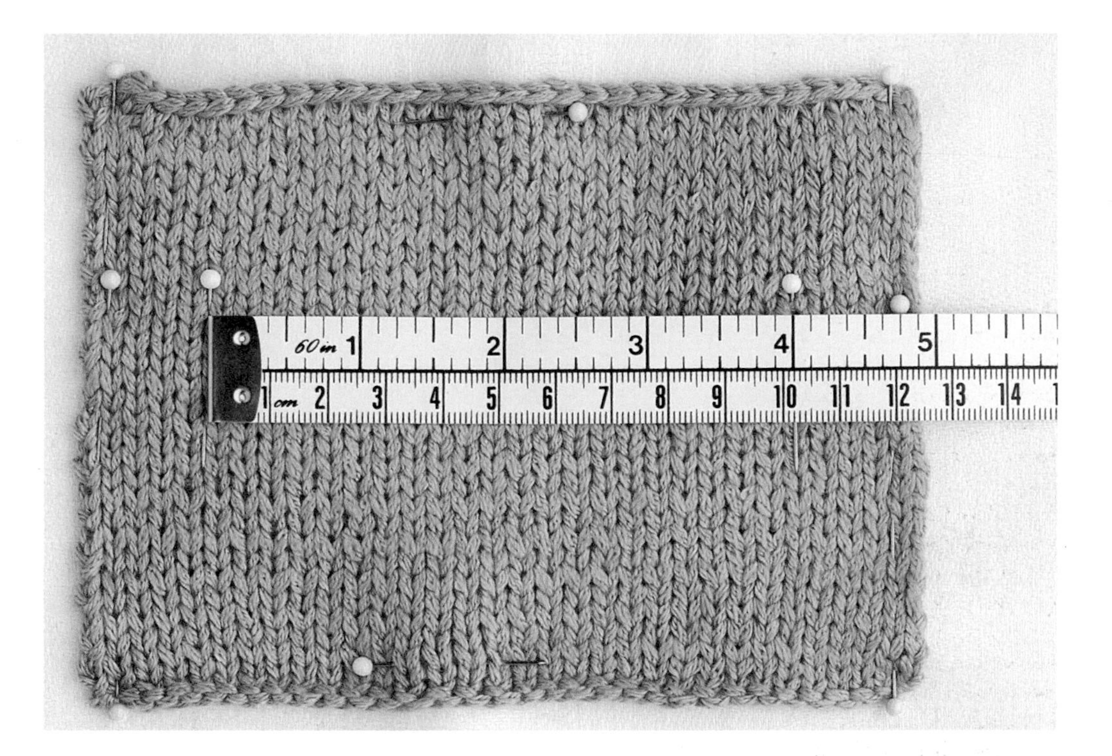

only takes a little time and it will make your toy turn out better.

I find that for toys it is better to be a little tighter than too loose because the stuffing tends to stretch the knitting a bit. Therefore, some tensions/gauges given in the patterns may be tighter than that on the ball band of the yarn.

measuring tension/gauge

To measure tension/gauge, first knit a swatch measuring at least 15 cm (6 in) square. This gives you plenty of room to accurately measure the number of stitches and rows over 10 cm (4 in) square. It can be hard to measure a smaller swatch accurately as the edges can curl up slightly. Flatten your knitting on a table top or pin it to your ironing board until it is flat. Steam press it or block it if required (see blocking, page 14).

To measure the stitch tension/gauge, use a ruler and pins to mark 10 cm (4 in) widthways across the middle of the knitted swatch. Count the number of stitches between the pins. To check the row tension/gauge, do the same but measure lengthways. If the number of stitches/rows is greater than that quoted in the pattern, your stitch size is too small. This can be remedied by using larger needles than those stated in the pattern. If the number of stitches/rows is fewer than that quoted in the pattern, your stitch size is too big and you need to use smaller needles. Keep doing tension/gauge squares, changing needle size as required, until you get the correct result.

When you begin to knit your toy you may find that with more stitches on the needles you are knitting more tightly or loosely. If you think this is happening, check your tension/gauge square against your toy and adjust the needle size if necessary.

finishing

Sewing up is going to make the difference between a professional -looking toy and a home made one, so take your time when finishing your toy.

Weaving in the ends is important: knotting the ends is not a good idea because the knot can slip to the front of the work and look messy. A quick way of weaving in ends is to weave a darning needle through the back of the knitting and then thread the end of yarn through the eye and pull it through the knitting. This prevents short ends from slipping out of the needle as you weave.

mattress stitch

Mattress stitch is the simplest seaming technique and produces a totally straight and invisible seam. It is especially useful when sewing up stripy knits. If backstitch is used, which entails pinning the pieces together with right sides facing, stripes can move out of alignment, but mattress stitch avoids pinning and is worked on the right side to achieve a perfect match.

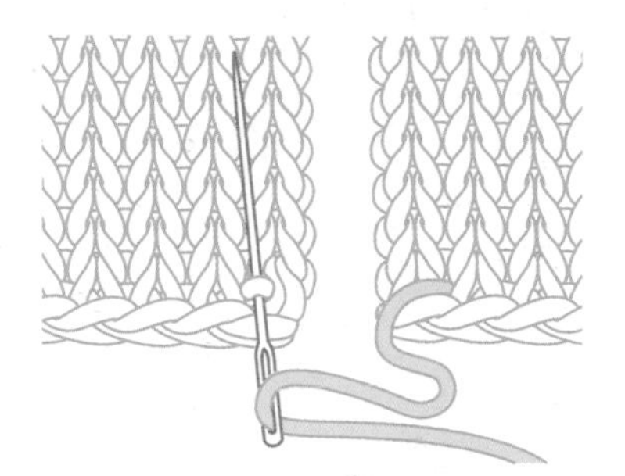

1 With the right sides of the knitted pieces facing you, insert a blunt-pointed knitter's sewing needle between the first and second stitches on the first row of the seam.

2 Then insert the needle into the other piece, in the centre of the second stitch in from the edge. Link the sides in a zigzag manner, as shown above.

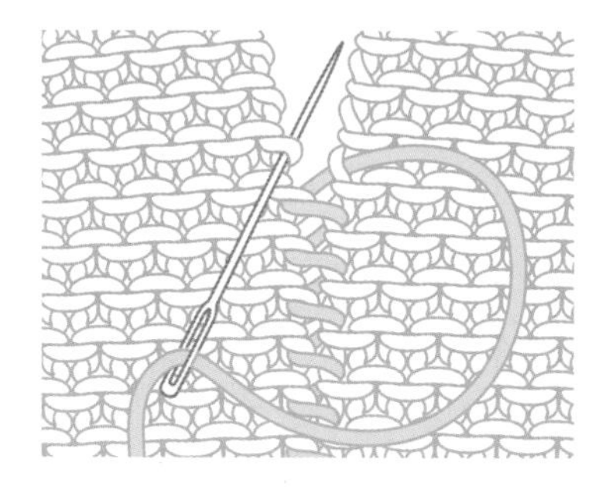

3 On garter stitch, work through the lower loop on one edge, then through the upper loop of the corresponding stitch on the other edge.

backstitch

Backstitch is good for tidying edges with lots of colour joins.

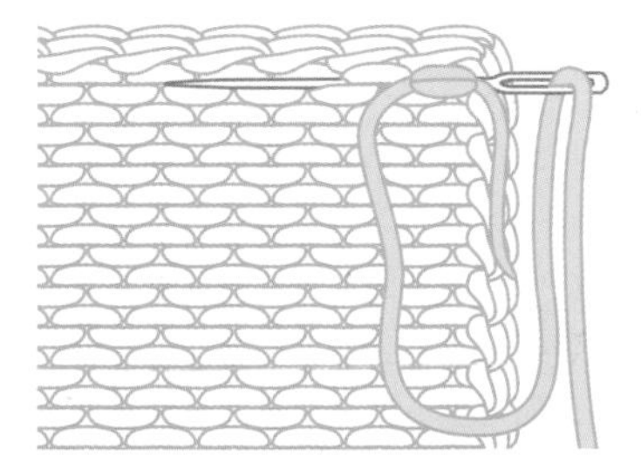

1 With the right sides together, secure the seam with a starting stitch. Bring the sewing needle through both pieces of knitting, making your first stitch about 1 cm (⅜ in) in size.

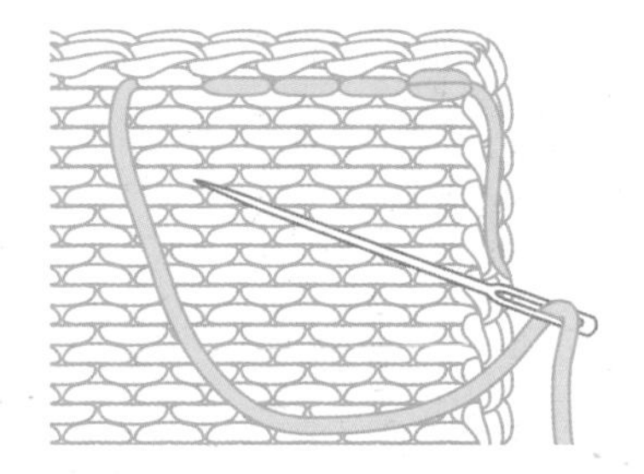

2 Then loop back to where the yarn came out of your stitch and bring the needle out a little past the end of the last stitch. Continue like this, taking the needle backward and forward with each stitch.

blocking

Blocking, or pressing, pieces of knitting before sewing the seams gives a more professional finish, as the edges will be flatter and not curl up. As you will stuff the toy this isn't essential, but if you want to make perfect seams you may wish to block your toy pieces.

Always check the yarn label for temperatures and to see if you can press directly onto your knitting. Most of the yarns I have chosen can be pressed, but if your yarn contains acrylic it may not be suitable.

To block your knitting, carefully pin each piece face down on a flat surface (see below) – I find the ironing board ideal. While pinning the pieces, gently nudge them into the desired shape without pulling the stitches too tightly. Then lightly press or steam the knitted fabric (on the back of the work) until it is flat. If you steam your knitting, remember to let it dry out completely before removing the pins.

edges and finishes

The finish and character of your toy will depend to an extent on the materials you decide to finish it with. I have used felt, which is available from most craft shops, to make ears and eyes with a more graphic and comical feel. I have also used buttons and embroidery for a more traditional and nostalgic look. Experiment with these materials and finishes to create your perfect toy. Remember to take your toy with you when choosing the finishing touches so that you get the exact look you're after.

Felt is a great fabric to use because it doesn't fray when cut and comes in a choice of bright and bold colours. Embroider faces onto toys before sewing them up completely, as it is easier to tie off the threads from the inside of the knitting and then sew up the toy.

pompoms

The bunny toy's tail and the bobble on the boy doll's hat are made from pompoms.

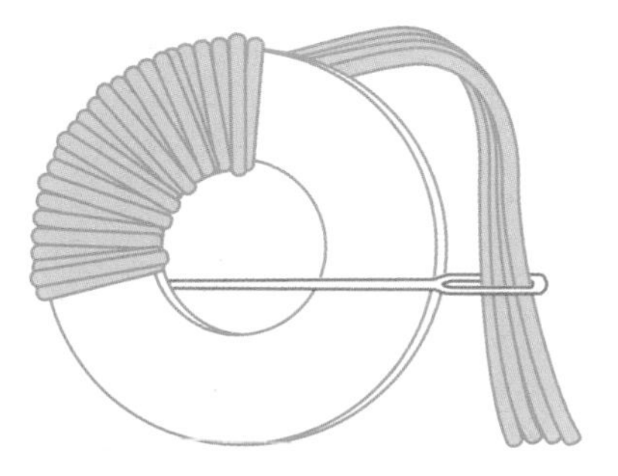

1 Cut two cardboard circles 5.5 cm (2¼ in) in diameter. Cut a central hole 2.5 cm (1 in) in diameter in each circle. Thread a knitter's sewing needle with two strands of yarn, each one 185 cm (72 in) long. Holding the circles together, pass the needle through the central hole, over the outside edge and through the central hole again to wrap the yarn around the circles. When you reach the end of the yarn, cut more strands and repeat until the circles are covered with yarn. Do not pull the yarn too tight.

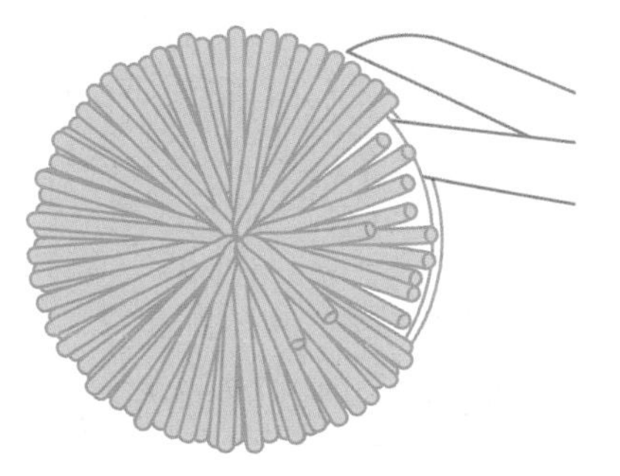

2 Using very sharp scissors, cut the yarn between the edges of the two circles.

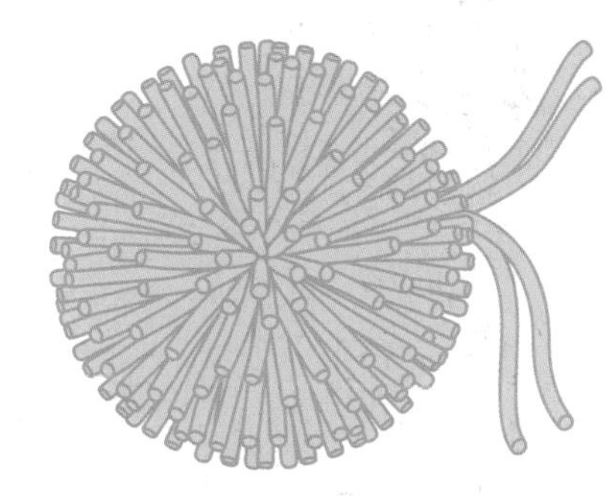

3 Cut a 60 cm (24 in) strand of yarn and double it. Slip the yarn between the cardboard circles, pull it up tightly and tie it firmly. Remove the cardboard circles and fluff out the pompom. Trim any protruding ends with scissors.

blanket stitch

The other finish I have used is blanket stitch. I used embroidery thread to do this as it is very colourful and not too thick. You could also use yarn, but this may look a bit chunky.

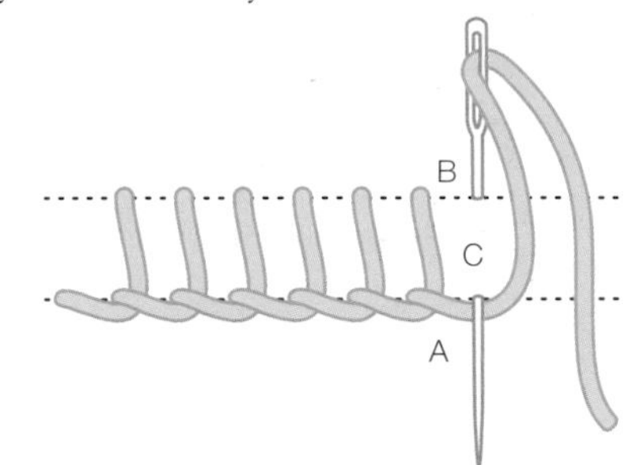

Work blanket stitch from left to right. From the back, bring the needle through the fabric at A. Take the needle from front to back to front in a single motion at B and C. Before pulling the needle through the fabric, wrap the embroidery thread under the point of the needle (see above). Where the needle comes out at C is point A of the next stitch.

felting

To felt yarn it is best to use 100% wool that is not suitable for machine-washing. (The machine-washable wools are usually treated or spun to ensure washability and avoid felting.)

Knit a piece at least 25% longer than the finished measurement of the toy. Felt it by machine-washing the swatch at 90°, using soap flakes. The extreme temperature and soap flakes will matt the woollen fibres, shrinking them together to make a tight, soft fabric that, when dry, can be cut without fraying. As the shrinking is quite severe, it is fine to knit the piece looser than you would if it were not to be shrunk. Experiment with different tensions/gauges to see how firm you like the felt to feel. If you have any leftover pieces of felted yarn, keep them to make ears or eyes on other toys.

abbreviations

( ) repeat enclosed instructions the number of times indicated.

approx. approximate(ly)

cm centimetre(s)

dec decrease by knitting/purling the next 2 stitches together

in inch(es)

inc increase by knitting into the front and back of the next stitch

k knit

k2tog knit the next 2 sts together

k2togb knit the next 2 sts together through the back loops

m1 make 1 stitch by picking up and working into back of loop between last st and next st

mm millimetre(s)

p purl

p2tog purl the next 2 stitches together

p2togb purl the next 2 stitches together through the back loops

p3tog purl the next 3 stitches together

psso pass the slipped stitch over

RS right side

s1 slip the next stitch

s1p slip the next stitch purlwise

skpo slip 1, knit 1, pass the slipped stitch over the knitted stitch

st(s) stitch(es)

stocking/stockinette stitch 1 row knit, 1 row purl. Repeat these 2 rows.

WS wrong side

yrn yarn round needle – wrap yarn around right needle from front to back and bring it to front again between needles to make a stitch

knitting pretty

dress-up dolly

This delightful dolly with her lovely pinafore dress and woolly plaits will enchant any little girl. Knit a few in different colour ways, then invite them all to a tea party.

size

Approx. 25 cm (10 in) tall

materials

Oddments of Jaeger Matchmaker Merino DK in **A** (mauve/Azalea 897) for shoes and tights, **B** (lilac/Parma 888) and **C** (fawn/Soft Camel 865) for skin and **D** (red/Cherry 656) for dress
Oddment of **E** (Black 681) for hair
Pair each of 3 mm (US 2/3) and 4 mm (US 6) knitting needles
Knitter's sewing needle
Washable stuffing
Embroidery needle
Red and green embroidery threads for face
Green and pink felt for flower in hair

tension/gauge

26 sts and 36 rows to 10 cm (4 in) square over stocking/stockinette stitch using 3 mm (US 2/3) needles.

abbreviations

See page 17.

legs (make 2)

Using 3 mm (US 2/3) needles and A, cast on 14sts.

1st row (K1, inc) 7 times. (21sts)

2nd row P.

3rd row K7, (inc, k1) 4 times, k6. (25sts)

4th-10th rows Stocking/stockinette stitch.

11th row K7, (skpo) twice, s1, k2tog, psso, (k2tog) twice, k7. (19sts)

12th row P.

13th row K2tog, k15, k2tog. (17sts)

14th-50th rows Change to B and work in stocking/stockinette stitch in 2-row stripes of B and A, (starting with a purl row). Cast/bind off.

Make second leg to match.

Weave in any loose ends. With RS facing join leg and shoe seams leaving cast/bound off edge open. Turn RS out. Stuff firmly and close opening.

body

Using 3 mm (US 2/3) needles and B, cast on 24 sts.

Work 2 rows in stocking/stockinette stitch. Mark 12th and 13th sts.

3rd row Using A, (k2, m1, k1) 8 times. (32sts)

4th row P.

5th-14th rows Work in stocking/stockinette stitch in 2-row stripes of B and A. Break yarns.

15th-26th rows Change to C, stocking/stockinette stitch.

shape shoulders

27th row K6, skpo, k2tog, k12, skpo, k2tog, k6.

28th row P.

29th row K5, skpo, k2tog, k10, skpo, k2tog, k5.

30th row P.

31st row K4, skpo, k2tog, k8, skpo, k2tog, k4.

32nd row P.

33rd row (K2, m1) to last 2sts, k2. (29sts)

Starting with a purl row, work 21 rows stocking/stockinette stitch.

shape top of head

1st row (K3, k2tog) to last 4sts, k4. (24sts)

2nd and 4th rows P.

3rd row (K3, k2tog) to last 4sts, k4. (20sts)
5th row (K1, k2tog) to last 2sts, k2. (14sts)
6th row (P2tog) across row.
Break yarn leaving 25 cm (10 in) end. Thread yarn through stitches and pull up tightly. Fasten securely. With RS together, join head seam and body seam. Turn RS out and stuff firmly. Close body opening, placing body seam to marker on cast on edge (making body seam at centre back).

arms (make 2)

Work in stocking/stockinette stitch.
Using 3 mm (US 2/3) needles and C, cast on 4sts.
1st row Inc in each stitch. (8sts)
2nd row P.
3rd row Inc, k2, (inc) twice, k2, inc.
4th row Inc, p9, inc, p1. (14sts)
5th-10th rows Stocking/stockinette stitch.
11th row Inc each end of row.
12th-34th rows Stocking/stockinette stitch.
Cast/bind off.
RS facing, join arm seam leaving cast/bound off edge open. Turn RS out and stuff. Close opening. Attach to body, having the seams on the underside of the arms and the top of the arms at the second shoulder decrease.

dress

Using 4 mm (US 6) needles and D cast on 50sts.
Work 4 rows in moss/seed stitch.
Change to stocking/stockinette stitch and work 26 rows, dec each end on 11th and 21st rows.
27th row (K1, p2tog) to last st, k1. (31sts)
28th-33rd rows Moss/seed stitch.
34th row Moss/seed stitch 6, cast/bind off 3sts, moss/seed stitch 13, cast/bind off 3sts, moss/seed stitch 6.

right back

On last 6sts work right back.
35th row Moss/seed stitch 4, dec.
36th-40th rows Moss/seed stitch.

shape neck

41st row Cast/bind off 2sts, moss/seed stitch to end.
42nd-45th rows Moss/seed stitch.
Cast/bind off.

front

On 13sts work front.
35th row RS facing, rejoin yarn, dec, moss/seed stitch 9, dec.
36th-37th rows Moss/seed stitch.
38th row Moss/seed stitch 3, cast/bind off 5sts, moss/seed stitch 3.
39th-45th rows On last 3sts, moss/seed stitch.
Cast/bind off.
On remaining 3sts work other side of front neck to match.

left back

On remaining 6sts work left back to match right back, reversing shapings.
Weave in any loose ends. With RS facing, join back and shoulder seams.

finishing

Attach legs to body.
Dress doll and stitch dress to body at shoulders if required.
Embroider face, see photograph.
Hair cut 30 cm (12 in) lengths of yarn E and stitch down using black thread. Make two plaits and stitch into place.
Cut out a felt flower and attach to hair.

airy fairy

A colourful modern fairy that's a perfect toy for a contemporary little girl. With her pretty net skirt and scalloped felt wings she will become a favourite play mate.

size

Approx. 25 cm (10 in) tall

materials

Oddments of Rowan Cotton Glace in **A** (purple/Hot Lips 818) for shoes, **B** (lilac/Hyacinth 787) and **C** (mauve/Tickle 811) for tights, **D** (green/Pier 809) for body, **E** (cream/Oyster 730) for skin and **F** (yellow/Butter 795) for hair
Pair of 3 mm (US 2/3) knitting needles
Knitter's sewing needle
Washable stuffing
Embroidery needle
Red and blue embroidery threads for face
Purple narrow ribbon for hair
Purple felt for wings
Purple net for skirt
Turquoise ribbon for skirt

tension/gauge

26 sts and 36 rows to 10 cm (4 in) square over stocking/stockinette stitch using 3 mm (US 2/3) needles.

abbreviations

See page 17.

legs

Using A, cast on 14sts.

1st row (K1, inc) 7 times. (21sts)

2nd row P.

3rd row K7, (inc, k1) 4 times, k6. (25sts)

4th–10th rows Stocking/stockinette stitch.

11th row K7, (skpo) twice, s1, k2tog, psso, (k2tog) twice, k7. (19sts)

12th row P.

13th row K2tog, k15, k2tog. (17sts)

14th–50th rows Change to B and C and work in stocking/stockinette stitch in 2-row stripes (starting with a purl row). Leave sts on spare needle. Break yarns. Make second leg to match but do not break yarns.

body

51st row Knit across second leg, then first leg. (34sts)

52nd–63rd rows Continue with stripe sequence in stocking/stockinette stitch. Break yarns.

64th–76th rows Change to D, stocking/stockinette stitch.

shape shoulders

1st row K6, skpo, k1, k2tog, k12, skpo, k1, k2tog, k6.

2nd and 4th rows P.

3rd row K5, skpo, k1, k2tog, k10, skpo, k1, k2tog, k5.

5th row K4, skpo, k2tog, k8, skpo, k1, k2tog, k4.

6th row Change to E, purl.

7th row (K2, m1) to last 2sts, k2. (32sts)

Starting with a purl row, work 21 rows stocking/stockinette stitch.

shape top of head

1st row (K3, k2tog) to last 2sts, k2. (2sts)

2nd and 4th rows P.

3rd row (K2, k2tog) to last 2sts, k2. (20sts)

5th row (K1, K2tog) to last 2sts, k2. (14sts)

6th row (P2tog) across row.

Break yarn leaving 25 cm (10 in) end. Thread yarn through stitches and pull up tightly. Fasten securely. Weave in any loose ends. With RS together, join head seam, join shoes and leg seams, then tights part of body. Turn RS out and stuff firmly. Close body opening.

arms (make 2)

Work in stocking/stockinette stitch.

Using E, cast on 4sts.

1st row Inc in each stitch. (8sts)

2nd row P.

3rd row Inc, k2, (inc) twice, k2, inc.

4th row Inc, p9, inc, p1. (14sts)

5th–10th rows Stocking/stockinette stitch.

11th row Change to D, inc each end of row.

12th–34th rows Stocking/stockinette stitch.

Cast/bind off.

Weave in any loose ends.

RS facing, join arm seam leaving cast/bound off edge open. Turn RS out and stuff. Close opening. Attach to body, having the seams on the underside of the arms and the top of the arms at the second shoulder decrease.

finishing

Embroider face, see photograph.

Hair using F, cut 23 cm (9 in) lengths and secure by sewing to top of head down centre parting. Trim ends and make a pony tail on each side of head. Tie pony tails with narrow ribbon.

Wings cut out of felt from template (see page 141) and sew on to back of body.

Skirt cut petal-shaped length of netting and sew around waist of fairy. Wrap ribbon around waist over top edge of net, tie a bow at the back and secure with tiny stitches.

cat pyjama case

With her dotty body and stripy tail this little cat looks so sweet curled up on a bed. With easy access at the back it's so useful for keeping your PJs nice and tidy too.

size

28 cm (11 in) wide x 23 cm (9 in) high

materials

3 50 g (1¾ oz) balls of Jaeger Extrafine Merino Aran in main colour **M** (light pink/Honesty 539) and 1 ball in **C** (dark pink/Pandora 551)

Pair of 4.5 mm (US 7) needles

Knitter's sewing needle

Washable stuffing

2 2.5 cm (1 in) buttons

Embroidery needle

Pink embroidery thread for face

Black and white felt for eyes

tension/gauge

19 sts and 25 rows to 10 cm (4 in) square over stocking/stockinette stitch using 4.5 mm (US 7) needles.

abbreviations

See page 17.

charts

See page 140.

front

Using M, cast on 16sts.

Working in stocking/stockinette stitch and using intarsia technique, follow Front chart.

back

part A

Using M, cast on 13sts.

Working in stocking/stockinette stitch with a moss/seed stitch border, follow Back A chart.

part B

Using M, cast on 13sts.

Working in stocking/stockinette stitch with a moss/seed stitch border, follow Back B chart, working buttonholes as indicated.

face (make 2)

Using M, cast on 13sts.

Working in stocking/stockinette stitch with moss/seed stitch ears, follow Face chart.

tail

Using M, cast on 18sts.

Work throughout in stocking/stockinette stitch stripes of 6 rows M, 6 rows C. Work 9 stripes.

stripe 10

1st row K.

2nd row (P2tog, p2) times, p2. (14sts)

3rd-6th rows Stocking/stockinette stitch.

stripe 11

1st row K.

2nd row P2tog, (p1, p2tog) four times. (9sts)

3rd-6th rows Stocking/stockinette stitch.

stripe 12

1st row K.

2nd row P1, (p2tog) 4 times. (5sts)

3rd row K.

4th row P.

5th row K2tog, k1, k2tog.

6th row P.

7th row Sl1, k2tog, psso. Fasten off.

finishing

Weave in any loose ends. Press pieces lightly using a warm iron over a damp cloth.

Body With RS together, pin front to backs ensuring that the moss/seed stitch edgings overlap. With the buttonhole edging in the middle of the 'sandwich', backstitch around edges. Turn RS out. Sew on buttons to match buttonholes.

Face With RS together, stitch around face leaving cast on edges open. Turn RS out and stuff lightly. Close cast on edges. Embroider face, see photograph. Attach to front of cat (see chart).

Eyes Cut felt shapes for eyes and sew down using thread.

Tail With RS together, stitch around tail leaving cast on edge open. Turn RS out and stuff lightly. Close opening. Attach to cat at lower seam (see chart).

face

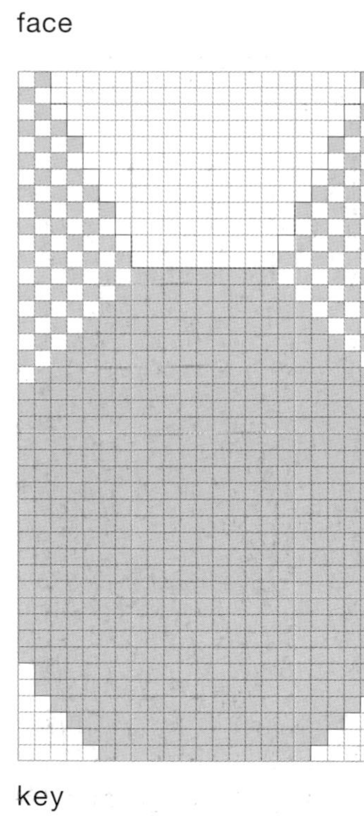

key

M

front

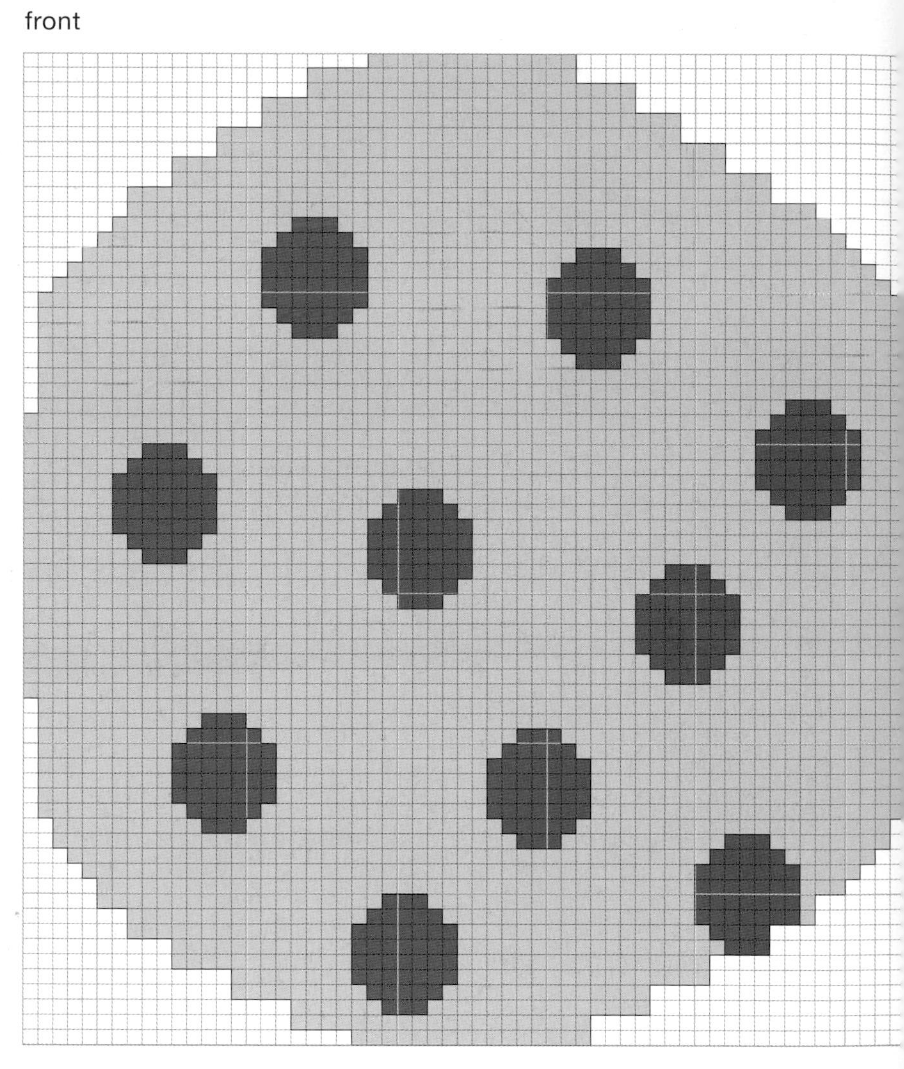

key

M

C

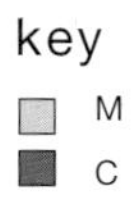

back A/back B

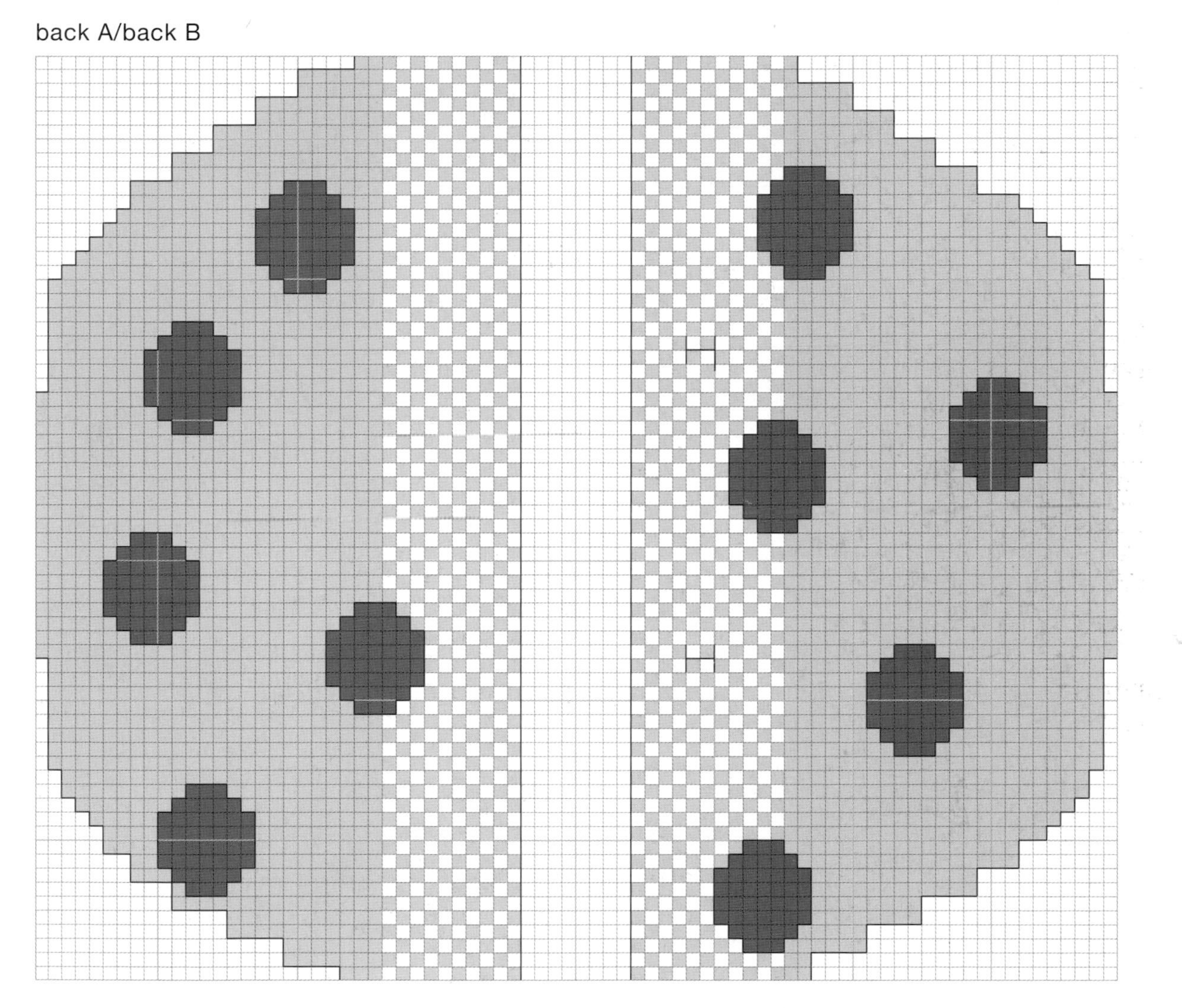

key

M

C

cow cushion

Daisy the cow has a comical grin and a dingley, dangley tail. She is happiest when tired little ones cuddle up to her and is perfect for bedtime reading.

size

33 cm (13 in) at widest point by 24 cm (9½ in) high

materials

3 50 g (1¾ oz) balls of Jaeger Matchmaker Merino DK in main colour **M** (White 661) and 1 ball in **B** (Black 681)

1 50 g (1¾ oz) ball of Rowan Wool Cotton in **A** (pale pink/Tender 951)

Pair of 3.75 mm (US 5) knitting needles

Safety pin

Knitter's sewing needle

Washable stuffing

Black and white felt for eyes

tension/gauge

23 sts and 35 rows to 10 cm (4 in) square over stocking/stockinette stitch using 3.75 mm (US 5) needles.

abbreviations

See page 17.

charts

See page 140.

body

part A

Using M, cast on 30sts.

Working in stocking/stockinette stitch and using intarsia technique, follow chart, working 1st row as a knit row and reading chart from right to left.

udder

With body RS facing and using A, pick up and knit 16sts between markers.

1st row P.

2nd row K to last 2sts, k2tog.

3rd row P.

4th row Dec each end.

5th-8th rows Work as 1st-4th rows.

9th row Dec each end. (8sts)

Leave sts on safety pin.

part B

Using M, cast on 30sts.

Working in stocking/stockinette stitch and using intarsia technique, follow chart, working 1st row as a purl row and reading chart from right to left.

udder

With body RS facing and using yarn A, pick up and knit 16sts between markers.

1st row P.

2nd row K2tog, knit to end.

3rd row P.

4th row Dec each end.

5th-8th rows Work as 1st-4th rows.

9th row Dec each end. (8sts)

Do not break yarn, leave sts on needle.

finishing udder

With WS of body pieces together, move 2sts from safety pin (part A) onto needle (part B). Using yarn A, k4, turn, p4, turn, k4, turn, p4, turn, (k2tog) twice, turn, p2tog. Fasten off.

Repeat * to * 3 more times.

With WS facing, carefully oversew side edge of teats.

face

part A

Using yarn A, cast on 10sts.

Working in stocking/stockinette stitch and using intarsia technique, follow chart, working 1st row as a knit row and reading chart from right to left.

part B

Using yarn A, cast on 10sts.

Working in stocking/stockinette stitch and using intarsia technique, follow chart, working 1st row as a purl row and reading chart from right to left.

legs (make 4)

Using B, cast on 8sts.

1st row (Inc) 8 times. (16sts)

2nd row P.

3rd-6th rows Stocking/stockinette stitch.

7th-36th rows Change to M, continue in stocking/stockinette stitch.

Cast/bind off.

face

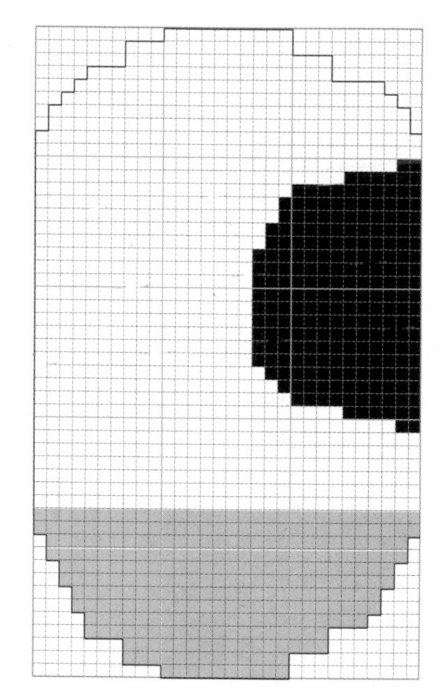

key

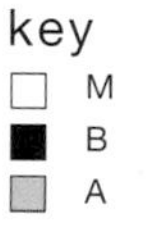

horns (make 2)

Using M, cast on 10sts.

1st–8th rows Stocking/stockinette stitch.

9th row K2tog, k2, (inc) twice, k2, k2tog.

10th row P.

11th–14th rows Work as 9th and 10th rows, twice. (10sts)

15th row K2tog, k6, k2tog.

16th row P.

17th and 18th rows Dec each end. (4sts)

19th row (K2tog) twice.

20th row P2tog, fasten off.

ears (make 2)

Using A, cast on 8sts.

Work 6 rows in stocking/stockinette stitch.

7th row Dec each end.

8th row P.

9th and 10th rows Work as 7th–8th rows. (4sts)

11th row Change to M, knit.

12th row Inc each end.

13th and 14th rows Work as 11th and 12th rows. (8sts)

15th–20th rows Stocking/stockinette stitch.

Cast/bind off.

tail

Cut 18 lengths of M, each 18 cm (7 in) long. Knot together at one end. Make a plait. Finish with a knot. Trim tail end.

finishing

Weave in any loose ends.

Body Pin tail into position and stitch to one piece of the body. Pin body pieces A and B together, RS facing. Sew around body leaving an opening for stuffing. Turn RS out. Lightly stuff and close opening. (You can use a 35 cm (14 in) round foam cushion pad trimmed to fit inside the body instead of the stuffing if you prefer.)

Face With RS facing, sew around face pieces A and B, leaving cast on edge open for stuffing. Turn RS out. Lightly stuff and close opening.

Horns With RS facing, join side seam, leaving cast on edge open for stuffing. Turn RS out. Lightly stuff. Attach to face, see chart.

Ears With RS facing, fold and join side seams, leaving cast on and cast/bound off edges open for stuffing. Turn RS out. Lightly stuff. Attach to face, see chart.

Eyes Cut felt shapes for eyes and sew down using thread. Stitch head to body.

Legs With RS facing, join side seam, leaving cast on edge open for stuffing. Turn RS out. Lightly stuff. Attach to body, see chart. Attach udder in same way.

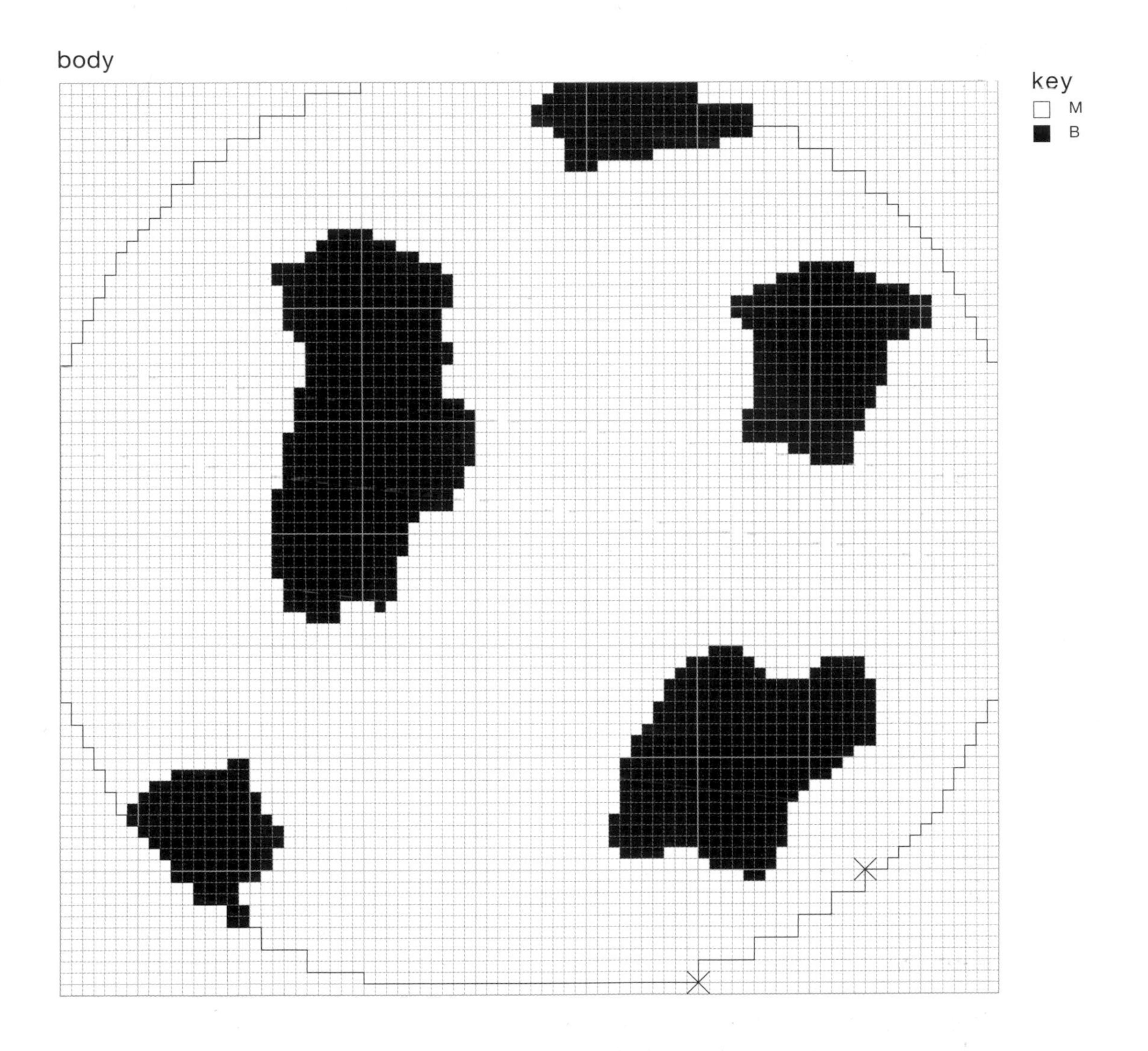
body
key
M
B

cot-hanger chick

A colourful chick to hang from the side of a cot and bring a smile to baby's face. These make perfect gifts for newborns and can easily be knitted in any colour way.

size

16 cm (6¼ in) wide and 13 cm (5 in) high

materials

1 50 g (1¾ oz) ball of Jaeger Baby Merino DK in yellow/Gold 225
Pair of 3 mm (US 2/3) knitting needles
Orange felt for wings and beak
Knitter's sewing needle
Washable stuffing
Yellow and orange felt for eyes
Embroidery needle
Yellow and orange embroidery threads

tension/gauge

28 sts and 36 rows to 10 cm (4 in) square over stocking/stockinette stitch using 3 mm (US 2/3) needles.

abbreviations

See page 17.

charts

See page 140.

side 1

Cast on 8sts.

Work from chart, starting with 1st row as a knit row and reading odd rows right to left and even rows left to right.

side 2

Work a mirror image of Side 1 by working from chart, but starting with 1st row as a purl row and reading odd rows right to left and even rows left to right.

finishing

Weave in any loose ends.

Cut 2 wings in felt. Attach to chick.

Cut 2 pieces for beak in felt. Attach to chick.

Place RS together and sew around chick, leaving an opening for stuffing. Turn RS out, stuff lightly and close opening.

Cut felt circles for eye and secure with a knot using embroidery thread.

Make a plait by plaiting 3 ends of yarn and 3 ends of orange embroidery thread to required length.

Note If you are hanging the chick near a small baby, please ensure that they can't tangle themselves up in the plait, or just make the plait short, to fasten to the cot bar.

side 1/side 2

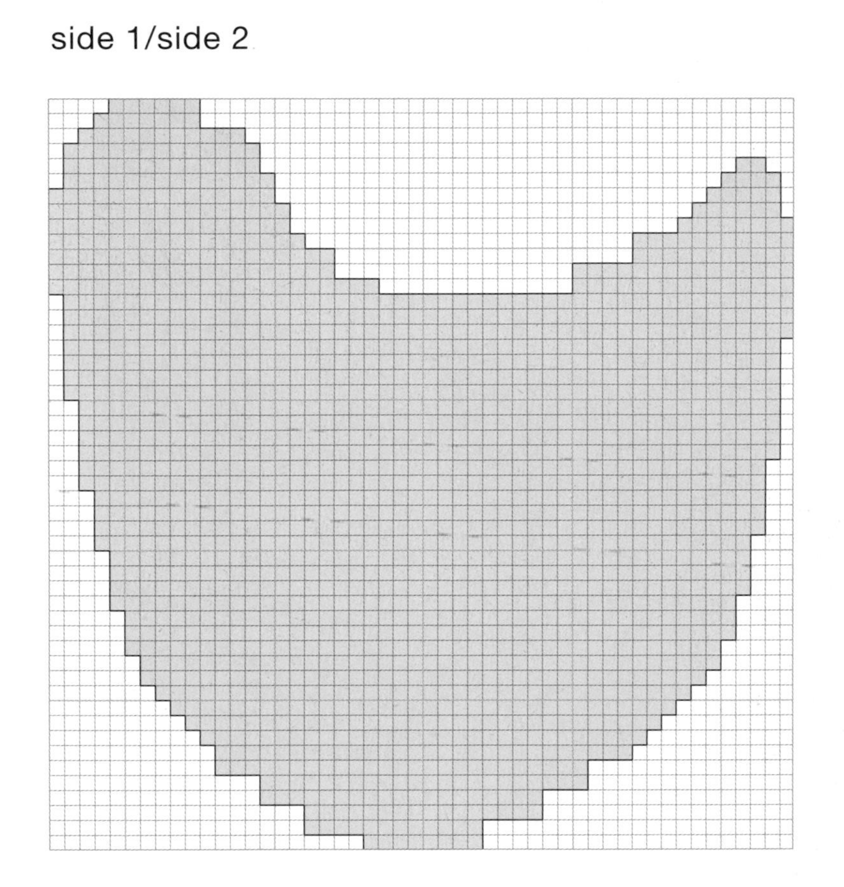

boy doll

Isn't it great to see a boy doll for a change? This little chap is set to become a firm friend for everyone with his soft fluffy hair and his cheeky smile.

size

Approx. 35 cm (14 in) tall

materials

1 50 g (1¾ oz) ball of Rowan Handknit Cotton DK in main colour **M** (Linen 205) for skin and **E** (green/Celery 309) for trousers. Small amounts in **A** (dark blue/Diana 287) and **B** (light blue/Ice Water 239) for sweater, **C** (white/Ecru 251) for boots, **D** (brown/Double Choc 315) for hat, and **F** (yellow/Buttercup 320) for hair

Pair each of 3.25 mm (US 3) and 4 mm (US 6) knitting needles

Knitter's sewing needle

Washable stuffing

Embroidery needle

Red and blue embroidery threads for face

tension/gauge

24 sts and 32 rows to 10 cm (4 in) square over stocking/stockinette stitch using 3.25 mm (US 3) needles.

abbreviations

See page 17.

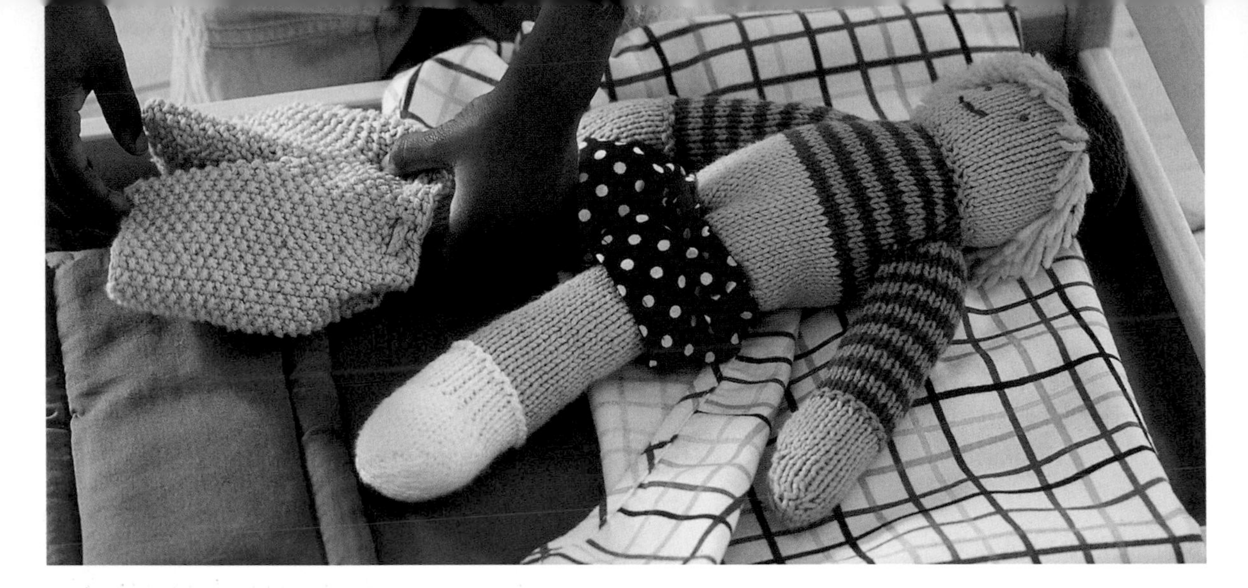

body

Using 3.25 mm (US 3) needles and M, cast on 44sts. Place marker between 22nd and 23rd sts.

1st row (WS) P.

2nd row K10, (m1, k1) twice, k20, (m1, k1) twice, k10. (48sts)

3rd-19th rows Stocking/stockinette stitch.

Change to A and B. Continue in stocking/stockinette stitch.

1st and 2nd rows A.

3rd and 4th rows B.

Keeping pattern of 2-row stripes of A and B, work as follows.

5th-10th rows Stocking/stockinette stitch.

11th row K9, (k2tog) 3 times, k18, (k2tog) 3 times, k9. (42sts)

12th-14th rows Stocking/stockinette stitch.

15th row K7, (k2tog) 3 times, k16, (k2tog) 3 times, k7. (36sts)

16th-18th rows Stocking/stockinette stitch.

19th row (K1, k2tog, k1) 9 times. (27sts)

20th row K.

Change to M.

1st row K.

2nd row P.

3rd row K1, (m1, k2) 13 times. (40sts)

4th-30th rows Stocking/stockinette stitch. Place marker at centre of 24th row for hat.

31st row (K3, k2tog) 8 times.

32nd row P.

33rd row (K2, k2tog) 8 times.

34th row P.

35th row (K1, k2tog) 8 times.

36th row (P2tog) 8 times.

Break yarn leaving a length for sewing. Thread yarn through remaining sts, pull together tightly and fasten.

Weave in any loose ends.

With RS together, sew back seam, leaving cast on edge open for stuffing.

arms (make 2)

Using 3.25 mm (US 3) needles and M, cast on 8sts.

1st row K.

2nd row (P1, inc) 3 times, p2.

3rd row K1, (inc, k2) 3 times, k1. (14sts)

4th-6th rows Stocking/stockinette stitch.

7th and 8th rows Cast on 2sts, work to end.

9th row K3, m1, k12, m1, k3. (20sts)

10th-16th rows Stocking/stockinette stitch.

Change to A and B.

17th and 18th rows B, knit.

19th row A, knit.

20th row A, purl.

21st-42nd rows Stocking/stockinette stitch in 2-row stripe pattern.

43rd and 44th rows Cast/bind off 2sts, work to end.
45th row K2tog, knit to last 2sts, k2tog.
46th row P.
47th row Work as row 45.
48th row (P2tog) 6 times.
Cast/bind off.

legs (make 2)

Using 3.25 mm (US 3) needles and C, cast on 24sts.
1st row (K1, inc) 12 times. (36sts)
2nd row P.
3rd-10th rows Stocking/stockinette stitch.
11th row K12, (k2tog) 6 times, k12. (30sts)
12th row P.
13th row K9, (k2tog) 6 times, k9. (24sts)
14th-20th rows Stocking/stockinette stitch.
21st and 22nd rows K.
23rd-52nd rows Change to M, work in stocking/stockinette stitch.
53rd row (K2tog, k8, k2tog) twice.
54th row P.
Cast/bind off.

hat

Using 4 mm (US 6) needles and D, cast on 40sts.
Knit 13 rows.
14th row (K3, k2tog) 8 times.
15th row K.
16th row (K2, k2tog) 8 times.
17th row K.
18th row (K1, k2tog) 8 times.
19th row (K2tog) 8 times.
Break yarn, leaving a length for sewing. Thread through remaining sts, pull together tightly and fasten off. Oversew back seam.
Make pompom (see page 15) to finish and sew on top.

trousers

first leg

*Using 4 mm (US 6) needles and E, cast on 29sts.
Work 20 rows in moss/seed stitch (every row [k1, p1] fourteen times, k1).* Break yarn. Leave sts on spare needle.

second leg

Work from * to * again. DO NOT BREAK YARN.
21st row Moss/seed stitch 29 (second leg), cast on 1st, moss/seed stitch 29 (first leg). (59sts)
22nd-38th rows Moss/seed stitch.
39th row (K1, yrn, k2tog, p1) to last 3sts, k1, yrn, k2tog.
40th and 41st rows Moss/seed stitch.
Cast/bind off in moss/seed stitch.

finishing

Weave in any loose ends.
Body Stuff firmly. Place back seam to marker at cast on edge. Oversew to close opening.
Head Sew hair under hat. Sew hat to head with back seam to back seam of head 5 rows up from sweater neck, and centre front of hat on marker.
Embroider eyes, nose and mouth, see photograph.
Arms With RS together, join underarm seam. Turn RS out and stuff firmly. Sew arms to body.
Legs With RS together, join back and foot seams. Turn RS out and stuff firmly. Sew legs to body.
Trousers With RS together, join leg seams and centre back seam. Turn RS out.
Tie belt Cut 6 50 cm (20 in) lengths of yarn E. Knot ends together. Make plait and knot the other end. Thread through eyelets at top of trousers.

squeaky pig

This clever piggy with his cute belly button and curly tail is sure to delight any child. This little piggy with a squeaker in his tummy squeaked all the way home.

size

Approx. 20 cm (8 in) tall

materials

1 50 g (1¾ oz) ball of Jaeger Baby Merino 4 ply in main colour **M** (pink/Magnolia 124), **A** (blue/Blue Ball 127) and **B** (ecru/Pearl 103)
Pair each of 3 mm (US 2/3) and 4 mm (US 6) knitting needles
Knitter's sewing needle
Washable stuffing
Squeaker
Embroidery needle
Blue embroidery thread for eyes

tension/gauge

25 sts and 38 rows to 10 cm (4 in) square over stocking/stockinette stitch using 3 mm (US 2/3) needles.

abbreviations

See page 17.

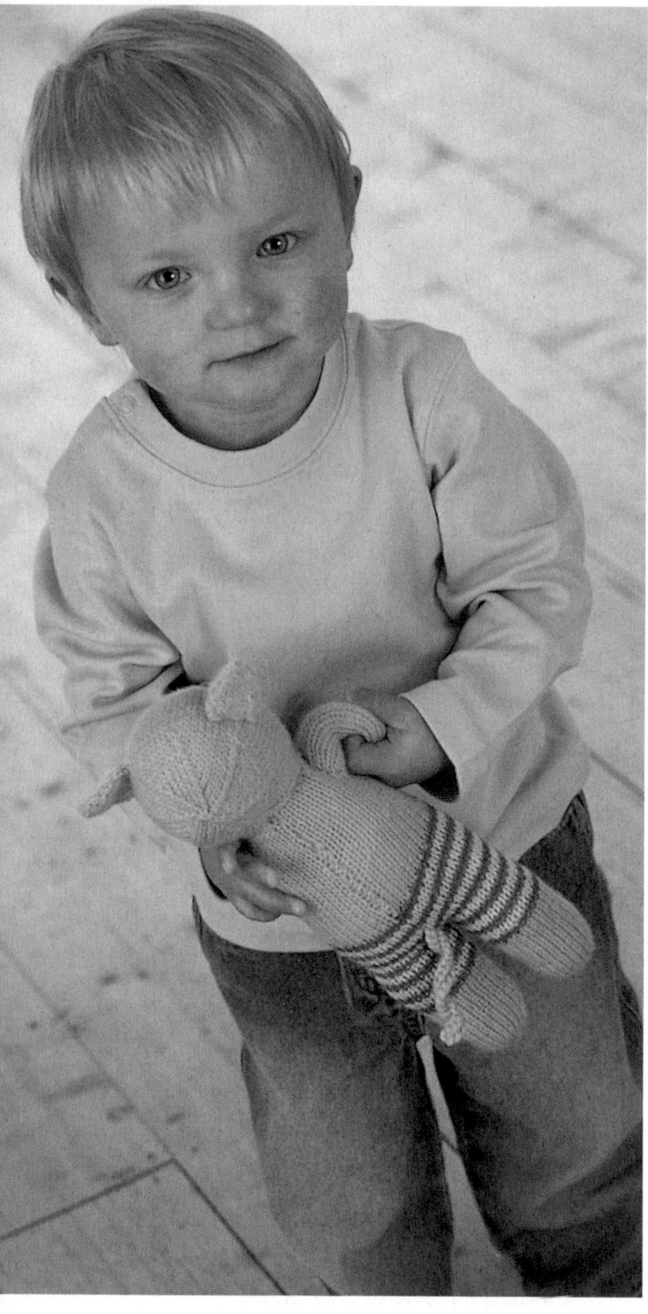

legs and body

first leg

Using 3 mm (US 2/3) needles and M, cast on 7sts.

1st row (Inc) 6 times, k1. (13sts)

2nd row (P1, inc) 6 times, p1. (19sts)

3rd row Inc, (k2, inc) 6 times. (26sts)

4th-22nd rows Stocking/stockinette stitch. Break yarn.

23rd-34th rows Work in stocking/stockinette stitch in 2-row stripes of A and B. Break yarns. Leave sts on spare needle.

second leg

Work rows 1-34 as first leg but do not break yarns A and B.

35th row Using A, knit across second leg, then first leg. (52sts)

body

36th row Using A, purl.

37th-48th rows Continue in 2-row stripes of A and B. Break yarns.

49th-68th rows Using M, stocking/stockinette stitch.

69th row K9, (k2tog) 4 times, k18, (k2tog) 4 times, k9. (44sts)

70th-76th rows Stocking/stockinette stitch.

77th row K7, (k2tog) 4 times, k14, (k2tog) 4 times, k7. (36sts)

78th row Purl, mark centre of row (neck).

Cast/bind off.

arms (make 2)

Using 3 mm (US 2/3) needles and M, cast on 9sts.

1st row Inc, k2, inc, k1, inc, k2, inc. (13sts)

2nd row Inc, purl to last st, inc.

3rd row Inc, knit to last st, inc.

4th row Work as row 2. (19sts)

5th-26th rows Stocking/stockinette stitch.

27th and 28th rows Cast/bind off 2sts, work to end.

29th row K2tog, knit to last 2sts, k2tog.

30th row P2tog, purl to last 2sts, p2tog.

Cast/bind off.

head

Start at nose.

Using 3 mm (US 2/3) needles and M, cast on 3sts.

1st row (Inc) twice, k1.

2nd row (Inc) 4 times, p1.

3rd row (K1, inc) 4 times, k1. (13sts)

4th-6th rows P.

7th-10th rows Stocking/stockinette stitch, starting with a knit row.

shape face

11th row (K1, m1) twice, knit to last 2sts, (m1, k1) twice. (17sts)

12th row and alt rows P.

13th row (K2, m1) 3 times, k5, (m1, k2) 3 times. (23sts)

15th row (K3, m1) 3 times, k5, (m1, k3) 3 times. (29sts)

17th row (K4, m1) 3 times, k5, (m1, k4) 3 times. (35sts)

Place markers at each end of row for chin.

19th row (K5, m1) 3 times, k5, (m1, k5) 3 times. (41sts)

21st row (K6, m1) 3 times, k5, (m1, k6) 3 times. (47sts)

23rd row (K7, m1) 3 times, k5, (m1, k7) 3 times. (53sts)

25th row K16, (m1, k2) 4 times, m1, k5, m1, (k2, m1) 4 times, k16. (63sts)

26th-38th rows Stocking/stockinette stitch. Place markers at each end of last row.

shape back of head

39th row (K7, k2tog) 7 times.

40th row and alt rows P.

41st row (K6, k2tog) 7 times.

43rd row (K5, k2tog) 7 times.

45th row (K4, k2tog) 7 times.

47th row (K3, k2tog) 7 times.

49th row (K2, k2tog) 7 times.

51st row (K1, k2tog) 7 times.

52nd row (P2tog) 7 times.

Break yarn leaving long end. Thread yarn through remaining sts, pull sts together tightly and fasten securely.

tail

Using 4 mm (US 6) needles and 2 ends of M, cast on 24sts. Cast/bind off tightly to make the knitting curl.

ears (make 2)

Using 3 mm (US 2/3) needles and M, cast on 8sts.

Work 24 rows in stocking/stockinette stitch, dec each end of 5th, 9th and 11th rows, inc each end of 13th, 15th and 19th rows.

Cast/bind off.

finishing

Weave in any loose ends.

Body With RS facing, join leg seams. Join trouser back seam, matching stripes and inserting tail at 4th/5th stripe down from waist. Join 4 cm (1½ in) seam from neck to trouser, leaving opening for stuffing.

Head With RS facing, join nose to marker and head shaping to marker. Turn RS out. Join head to body. With RS together, pin nose seam to marked centre of neck and back head seam to centre back. Pin head to neck cast/bound off. Stitch seams. Turn RS out and embroider tummy button using yarn M. Stuff firmly, placing squeaker in tummy area. Close back opening.

Arms With RS facing, join arm seams, leaving armhole shaping open. Turn RS out and stuff firmly. Attach arms to body, adding extra stuffing if required.

Ears With WS together oversew side seams.

Eyes Embroider eyes, see photograph.

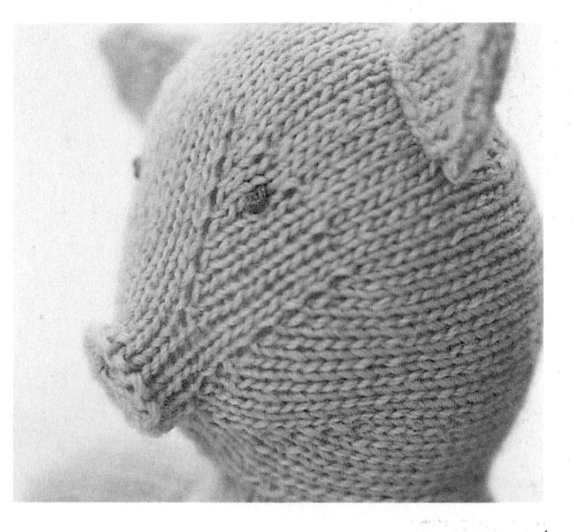

finger puppets

Bring your child's imagination alive with hours of fun telling stories with the help of these puppets. They're quick and easy to knit and great for using up left over yarns.

size

Approx. 9 cm (3½ in) tall

materials

Small amounts of Jaeger Matchmaker Merino 4ply for bears in soft green/Thyme 715, gold/Gold 756 and pale brown/Heath 754

Small amounts of Jaeger Baby Merino 4 ply for Goldilocks in **A** (red/Red Cheek 094), **B** (pink/Princess 126), **C** (ecru/Pearl 103) and **D** (yellow/Buttermilk 105)

Pair of 2.75 mm (US 2) knitting needles

Knitter's sewing needle

Small amount of washable stuffing

Embroidery needle

Blue and red embroidery threads for faces

Brown felt for bears' ears

tension/gauge

26 sts and 38 rows to 10 cm (4 in) square over stocking/stockinette stitch using 2.75 mm (US 2) needles.

abbreviations

See page 17.

papa bear

Using brown/Heath 754, cast on 24sts and knit 4 rows. Change to stocking/stockinette stitch and work 18 rows.

***19th row** (K2, k2tog) 6 times. (18sts)

20th-22nd rows Stocking/stockinette stitch.

23rd row K7, (m1, k1) 4 times, m1, k7. (23sts)

24th-26th rows Stocking/stockinette stitch.

27th row K9, skpo, k1, k2tog, k9.

28th row P9, p3tog, p9. (19sts)

29th-32nd rows Stocking/stockinette stitch.

33rd row (K1, k2tog) 6 times, k1.

34th row P.

35th row (K2tog) 6 times, k1.

Break yarn, leaving length for sewing. Thread yarn through remaining sts and secure firmly. Weave in any loose ends. With RS together, sew back seam. Turn RS out.*

arms (make 2)

Cast on 2sts.

1st row Inc in each stitch.

2nd row P.

3rd row (Inc) 3 times, k1.

4th-14th rows Stocking/stockinette stitch.

Cast/bind off. With RS together, join underarm seam. Turn RS out, stuff lightly and close opening.

mama bear

Using gold/Gold 756, cast on 24sts and work 6 rows in moss/seed stitch.

Change to stocking/stockinette stitch and work 14 rows.

Work from * to* as for Papa Bear.

arms (make 2)

Work as for Papa Bear.

baby bear

Using soft green/Thyme 715, cast on 22sts and work 6 rows in k1, p1 rib.

Change to stocking/stockinette stitch and work 14 rows.

15th row (K2, k2tog) 5 times, k2. (17sts)

16th-18th rows Stocking/stockinette stitch.

19th row K7, (m1, k1) 3 times, m1, k7. (21sts)

20th-22nd rows Stocking/stockinette stitch.

23rd row K8, skpo, k1, k2tog, k8.

24th row P8, p3tog, p8. (17sts)

25th and 26th rows Stocking/stockinette stitch.

27th row K1, (k1, k2tog) five times, k1.

28th row P.

29th row (K2tog) 6 times.

Break yarn, leaving length for sewing. Pull thread through remaining sts and secure firmly. Weave in any loose ends. With RS together, sew back seam. Turn RS out.

arms (make 2)

Work as for Papa Bear.

goldilocks

Using A, cast on 24sts and work 4 rows in moss/seed stitch.

Change to stocking/stockinette stitch and work 14 rows in 2-row stripes of B and A.

15th row Using A, (k2, k2tog) 6 times. (18sts)

16th row P.

17th row Change to C, knit.

18th row P.

19th row (K2, m1, k1) 6 times. (24sts)

20th-28th rows Stocking/stockinette stitch.

29th row (K1, k2tog) 8 times.

30th row (P2tog) 8 times.

Break yarn, leaving length for sewing. Pull thread through remaining sts and secure firmly. Weave in any loose ends. With RS together, sew back seam. Turn RS out.

arms (make 2)

Work as for Papa Bear using C.

finishing

Stuff head sections. Embroider faces on bears and Goldilocks, see photograph. Cut a pair of ears for each bear out of felt and sew into place. Cut lengths of yarn D for Goldilocks' hair and attach it to centre of her head. Make two bunches to finish her hairstyle.

fun favourites

shiny robot

With his squishy body and felt face, this robot is a great toy for the smallest child. You can easily experiment with his features to make a whole team of little robot friends.

size

Approx. 22 cm (8¾ in) tall

materials

1 25 g (1 oz) ball of Rowan Lurex Shimmer in main colour **M** (silver/Pewter 333)
Small amounts of Jaeger Siena 4ply in **A** (red/Chilli 425) and **B** (green/Salad 427)
Pair of 2.75 mm (US 2) knitting needles
Knitter's sewing needle
Washable stuffing
Green felt for eyes
Embroidery needle
Red embroidery thread for mouth

tension/gauge

30 sts and 42 rows to 10 cm (4 in) square over stocking/stockinette stitch using 2.75 mm (US 2) needles.

abbreviations

See page 17.

body

Start at lower edge.

Using M, cast on 30sts.

Work 14 rows in stocking/stockinette stitch.

15th row Cast on 40sts, knit.

16th row Cast on 10sts, purl. (80sts)

19th-38th rows Stocking/stockinette stitch.

39th row K47M, 16A, 17M.

40th row P17M, 16A, 47M.

41st and 42nd rows Work as 39th and 40th rows.

43rd-46th rows Work as 39th-42nd rows using B for A.

47th and 48th rows Work as 39th and 40th rows.

49th and 50th rows Work as 43rd and 44th rows.

Break yarns A and B.

51st-62nd rows Using M, stocking/stockinette stitch.

63rd row Cast/bind off 40sts, knit to end.

64th row Cast/bind off 10sts, purl to end.

65th-78th rows Stocking/stockinette stitch.

Cast/bind off.

head

Using M, cast on 20sts.

Work 10 rows in stocking/stockinette stitch.

11th row Cast on 26sts, knit to end.

12th row Cast on 6sts, purl to end. (52sts)

13th-26th rows Stocking/stockinette stitch.

27th row Cast/bind off 26sts, knit to end.

28th row Cast/bind off 6sts, purl to end.

29th-36th rows Stocking/stockinette stitch.

Cast/bind off.

arms (make 2)

Using M, cast on 4sts.

1st row (Inc) 4 times.

2nd row (Inc) 8 times. (16sts)

3rd row K.

4th-31st rows Stocking/stockinette stitch, starting with a knit row.

Cast/bind off.

legs (make 2)

Using M, cast on 5sts.

1st row (Inc) 5 times.

2nd row (Inc) 10 times. (20sts)

3rd and 4th rows K.

5th-16th rows Stocking/stockinette stitch.

17th and 18th rows Using A, knit.

19th-24th rows Using M, stocking/stockinette stitch.

25th and 26th rows Using B, knit.

27th-40th rows Using M, stocking/stockinette stitch.

Cast/bind off.

finishing

Weave in any loose ends.

Body With RS together, join side seam. Pin lower edge flap (cast on edge) to main part to make a rectangle. Turn RS out.

Head Work as for body.

Arms and legs With RS together and starting at cast/bound off edge, join seam, secure firmly, then run thread around cast on edge, pull together tightly and fasten off securely. Turn RS out.

Stuff all parts and sew together. Cut felt eyes and attach using cross stitch. Embroider mouth, see photograph.

flat ted

This teddy would make a great christening present. Make a blue one for a boy or soft pink for a girl, or just knit a plain brown one for a traditional look.

size

Approx. 36 cm (14½ in) tall

materials

1 50 g (1¾ oz) ball of Rowan Soft Baby in **A** (pink/Princess 003) and **B** (white/Cloud 001)
Pair of 4 mm (US 6) knitting needles
2 safety pins
Knitter's sewing needle
Washable stuffing
Embroidery needle
Pink embroidery thread for face
Pink and white felt for eyes

tension/gauge

22 sts and 28 rows to 10 cm (4 in) square over stocking/stockinette stitch using 4 mm (US 6) needles.

abbreviations

See page 17.

legs

first leg

Using A, cast on 12sts.

1st row Inc in each stitch.

2nd row P.

3rd row (K1, m1, k2) 8 times. (32sts)

4th row P.

5th–8th rows Using B, stocking/stockinette stitch.

9th row Using A, knit.

10th row (P1, p2tog, p1) 8 times. (24sts)

11th and 12th rows Stocking/stockinette stitch.

13th–40th rows Using B, continue in stocking/stockinette stitch in 4-row stripes of A and B.

Break yarn, leave sts on spare needle.

Make second leg to match. DO NOT BREAK YARN.

body

41st row Using A, knit across second leg then first leg. (48sts)

42nd–88th rows Continue in stocking/stockinette stitch in 4-row stripes of A and B. Break B.

89th row Using A, knit.

90th row P.

91st row (K1, k2tog, k1) 12 times. (36sts)

92nd row P.

head

93rd row K31, turn, place remaining 5sts on safety pin.

94th row P26, turn, place remaining 5sts on safety pin.

95th row K13, m1, k13.

96th row Inc, purl to last 2 sts, inc, p1.

97th row K14, m1, k1, m1, k14.

98th row and alt rows Work as 96th row.

99th row K16, m1, k1, m1, k16.

101st row K18, m1, k1, m1, k18.

103rd row K20, m1, k1, m1, k20.

105th row K22, m1, k1, m1, k22. (47sts)

106th–109th rows Stocking/stockinette stitch.

110th row P23, cast/bind off 1st, p23.

111th row On 23sts, k21, k2tog.

112th row P2tog, p20.

113th row K19, k2tog.
114th row P.
115th row K18, k2tog.
116th row P2tog, p17.
117th row K16, k2tog.
118th row P.
119th row Skpo, k13, k2tog.
120th row P2tog, p11, p2tog.
121st row Skpo, k9, k2tog.
122nd-123rd rows Cast/bind off 3sts, work to end.
124th row Cast/bind off.
With RS facing, rejoin yarn to remaining 23sts and work 111-121st rows, reversing shaping, (eg: 111th row, Skpo, k21).
122-124th rows Work as first side.
Place sts on safety pins back onto needle. (10sts)
With RS facing, rejoin A and work as follows.
1st row K.
2nd row Inc, purl to last 2sts, inc, p1.
3rd-10th rows Work as 1st and 2nd rows 4 times. (20sts)
11th-20th rows Stocking/stockinette stitch.
21st row K2tog, knit to last 2sts, skpo.
22nd-30th rows Stocking stitch.
31st row Work as 21st row.
32nd-36th rows Stocking/stockinette stitch.
37th row Work as 21st row.
38th row P.
39th and 40th rows Work as 37th and 38th rows.
41st row Work as 21st row.
42nd row P2tog, purl to last 2sts, p2tog.
43rd and 44th rows Work as 41st and 42nd rows.
45th row Work as 21st row.
46th row P2tog, fasten off.

arms (make 2)

Using A, cast on 6sts.
1st row (Inc) 6 times.
2nd row P.
3rd row (Inc, k1) 6 times. (18sts)
4th-8th rows Stocking/stockinette stitch.
9th row Using B, knit.
10th-36th rows Continue in stocking/stockinette stitch in 4-row stripes as on body.
Cast/bind off.

ears (make 2)

Using A, cast on 10sts.
1st-3rd rows Stocking/stockinette stitch.
4th row P2tog, p6, p2tog.
5th row K.
6th row P2tog, p4, p2tog. (6sts)
7th row K.
8th row (K1, p1) three times.
9th row Inc, (k1, p1) twice, inc.
10th-14th rows Moss/seed stitch.
Cast/bind off in moss/seed stitch.

finishing

Weave in any loose ends.
Body With RS together, join leg and foot seams. Ease back head piece around front head piece, pin and sew. Join body seam, leaving an opening for stuffing. Turn RS out and stuff. Close opening.
Arms With RS together, sew arm seam, leaving cast/bound off edge open. Turn RS out and stuff. Close opening and attach arms to body.
Ears With WS together, oversew side seams carefully. Attach ears to head. Cut felt eyes and attach as in photograph. Embroider face.

gingerbread man

Run, run as fast as you can, you can't catch this cute gingerbread man! With his smiley face and button eyes he's almost good enough to eat.

size

23 cm (9 in) tall

materials

2 25 g (1 oz) balls of Rowan Harris 4ply in Rust 009
Pair of 3.25 mm (US 3) knitting needles
Knitter's sewing needle
Washable stuffing
Embroidery needle
Red and orange embroidery threads for mouth and blanket stitching
5 1 cm (⅜ in) black buttons.

tension/gauge

26 sts and 38 rows to 10 cm (4 in) square over stocking/stockinette stitch using 3.25 mm (US 3) needles.

abbreviations

See page 17.

to make

Cast on 80sts and work 45 cm (18 in) in stocking/stockinette stitch. Cast/bind off.
Boil wash knitted oblong using soap flakes so that the fabric is felted. Allow to dry.
Cut around gingerbread man template (see page 141) twice, cutting one piece with the right side up and the other with the reverse side up to make the back and front of the gingerbread man.

finishing

RS facing, stitch pieces together, leaving a gap for stuffing. Stuff lightly and sew up edge. Embroider mouth and attach buttons for eyes and down centre front of gingerbread man, see photograph. Complete by blanket stitching around shape using embroidery thread.

big-foot bunny

This bouncing bunny with his oversized feet will look sweet in any child's bedroom. This classic toy with a modern twist is sure to appeal to children both big and small.

size

Approx. 32 cm (12¾ in) tall

materials

2 50g (1¾ oz) balls of Rowan All Seasons Cotton in main colour **M** (turquoise/Jazz 185), and 1 ball in **C** (lime green/Lime Leaf 217)
Pair of 4 mm (US 6) knitting needles
Safety pin
Knitter's sewing needle
Washable stuffing
Blue embroidery thread for face
Lime green velvet ribbon

tension/gauge

20 sts and 28 rows to 10 cm (4 in) square over stocking/stockinette stitch using 4 mm (US 6) needles.

abbreviations

See page 17.

body and head

Start at lower edge.

Using M, cast on 16sts.

1st row (WS) and alt rows Purl.

2nd row K3, m1, k2, m1, (k3, m1) twice, k2, m1, k3. (21sts)

4th row K1, m1, k3, m1, k2, m1, k4, m1, k1, m1, k4, m1, k2, m1, k3, m1, k1. (29sts)

6th row K.

8th row K6, m1, k2, m1, k13, m1, k2, m1, k6. (33sts)

10th row K.

12th row K2, m1, k5, m1, k2, m1, k6, m1, k3, m1, k6, m1, k2, m1, k5, m1, k2. (41sts)

13th-39th rows Stocking/stockinette stitch.

shape top of body

40th row (K3, k2tog) twice, (skpo, k3) twice, k1, (k3, k2tog) twice, (skpo, k3) twice. (33sts)

41st-43rd rows Stocking/stockinette stitch.

44th row (K2, k2tog) twice, (skpo, k2) twice, k1, (k2, k2tog) twice, (skpo, k2) twice. (25sts)

45th-47th rows Stocking/stockinette stitch.

shape head

1st row K12, m1, k1, m1, k12. (27sts)

2nd row P.

3rd row (K2, m1, k3, m1) twice, k2, m1, (k1, m1) three times, k2, (m1, k3, m1, k2) twice. (39sts)

4th row P.

5th row K18, (m1, k1) three times, m1, k18. (43sts)

6th-10th rows Stocking/stockinette stitch.

11th row K19, k2tog, k1, skpo, k19.

12th row P18, p2togb, p1, p2tog, p18.

13th row K17, k2tog, k1, skpo, k17.

14th row P.

15th row K16, k2tog, k1, skpo, k16. (35sts)

16th-24th rows Stocking/stockinette stitch.

shape top of head

25th row (K3, k2tog) 7 times.

26th row P.

27th row (K2, k2tog) 7 times.

28th row P.

29th row (K1, k2tog) 7 times.

30th row (K2tog) 7 times.

Break yarn, leaving a length for sewing. Thread yarn through remaining sts, pull together and secure firmly. With RS together, sew back seam leaving cast on edge open.

feet and legs

Start at toe.

Using M, cast on 5sts.

1st row K1, (inc) 3 times, k1.

2nd row P.

3rd row K3, m1, k2, m1, k3.

4th row P.

5th row (K2, m1) 4 times, k2.

6th-23rd rows Stocking/stockinette stitch.

24th row P5, turn and work 8 rows stocking/stockinette stitch on these sts. Cast/bind off. (Heel).

Next row WS facing, slip next 4sts onto safety pin, rejoin yarn, p5. Work 8 rows on these 5sts. Cast/bind off. (Heel).

Next row RS facing, pick up 8sts from heel to safety pin, k4sts from safety pin, pick up 8sts from safety pin to heel. (20sts)

1st row P.

2nd row K6, skpo, k4, k2tog, k6.

3rd-23rd rows Stocking/stockinette stitch.

Cast/bind off.

Make second foot and leg to match.

arms

Using M, cast on 6sts.

1st row (Inc, k1) 3 times.

2nd row P.

3rd row K1, m1, k2, m1, k3, m1, k2, m1, k1.

4th row P.

5th row (K3, m1) twice, k1, (m1, k3) twice. (17sts)

6th-30th rows Stocking/stockinette stitch.

31st and 32nd rows Cast/bind off 3sts, work to end.

33rd-35th rows Dec each end.

36th row P.

Cast/bind off.

ears

outer ear (make 2)

Using M, cast on 8sts.

Work 30 rows in stocking/stockinette stitch, inc each end of 5th and 11th rows, and dec each end of 21st, 25th and 27th rows. Cast/bind off.

inner ear (make 2)

Using C, cast on 5sts.

Work 26 rows in stocking/stockinette stitch, inc each end of 5th and 11th rows and dec each end of 21st, 23rd and 25th rows. Cast/bind off.

soles (make 2)

Start at toe end.

Using C, cast on 3sts.

1st row (Inc) twice, k1.

2nd row P.

3rd row K1, m1, k3, m1, k1.

4th row P.

5th row K2, m1, k3, m1, k2.

6th row P.

7th row (K3, m1) twice, k3. (11sts)

8th-24th rows Stocking/stockinette stitch.

25th row K2tog, knit to last 2sts, k2tog.

26th row P.

27th row Work as row 25.

28th row P2tog, purl to last 2sts, p2tog.

Cast/bind off.

finishing

Weave in any loose ends.

Legs With RS together, join leg seam. Insert sole and stitch into position. Turn RS out and stuff firmly, close cast/bound off edge.

Arms With RS together, join arm seam. Turn RS out and stuff firmly.

Body Stuff firmly and close lower edge; make sure that seam to head is at centre back. Attach legs to lower edge. Attach arms to body, adding stuffing if necessary.

Ears Place an inner and outer ear RS together, matching the increase rows. Ease remainder of outer ear around inner ear and stitch, leaving cast on edge open. Turn RS out. Attach to head.

Face Embroider face, see photograph. Make pompom (see page 15) from yarn M for tail and sew on. Tie ribbon around neck and stitch in place if preferred.

cheeky monkey

Sure to be a firm favourite with all cheeky little monkeys, his long arms mean he can hang around with you wherever you might be.

size

Approx. 62 cm (24¾in) tall

materials

3 50 g (1¾oz) balls of Rowan Yorkshire Tweed DK in **A** (blue/Slosh 345) and 1 ball in **B** (green 347/Skip) and **C** (ecru/Goose 352)

Pair of 3 mm (US 2/3) knitting needles

Knitter's sewing needle

Washable stuffing

Embroidery needle

Black felt for eyes

tension/gauge

28 sts and 36 rows to 10 cm (4in) square over stocking/stockinette stitch using 3 mm (US 2/3) needles.

abbreviations

See page 17.

charts

See page 140.

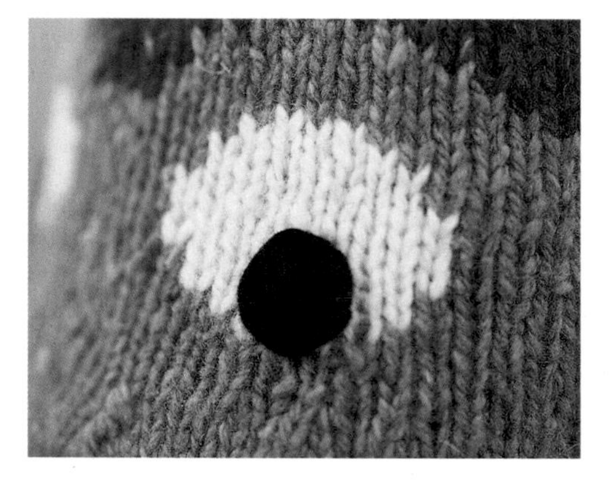

body and head

Start at lower edge of body.

Using A, cast on 36sts.

1st row (WS) P.

2nd row Inc, (k3, m1) 11 times, k2. (48sts)

3rd row P.

4th row K2, m1, (k4, m1) 11 times, k2. (60sts)

5th-7th rows Stocking/stockinette stitch.

8th row K3, m1, (k5, m1) 11 times, k2. (72sts)

9th-11th rows Stocking/stockinette stitch.

12th row K13, m1, k10, m1, k26, m1, k10, m1, k13.

13th-15th rows Stocking/stockinette stitch.

16th row K14, m1, k10, m1, k28, m1, k10, m1, k14.

17th-19th rows Stocking/stockinette stitch.

20th row K15, m1, k10, m1, k30, m1, k10, m1, k15. (84sts)

Continue in stocking/stockinette stitch, without shaping, until work measures 18 cm (7 in), ending with a purl row.

shape top of body

1st row (K2, k2tog, k3) to end. (72sts)

2nd-4th rows Stocking/stockinette stitch.

5th row (K2, k2tog, k2) to end. (60sts)

6th-8th rows Stocking/stockinette stitch.

9th row (K2, k2tog, k1) to end. (48sts)

10th-13th rows Stocking/stockinette stitch.

Use intarsia method from this point.

14th row WS facing, purl 10A, 28B, 10A.

start chin shaping

1st row Knit 10A, using B, k4, (m1, k2) 10 times, ml, turn, s1, p30, turn.

2nd row S1, k4, (m1, k3) 6 times, m1, k5, turn, s1, p31, turn.

3rd row S1, k24, turn, s1, p17, turn.

4th row S1, k12, turn, s1, p7, turn.

5th row S1, knit 26B, 10A.

6th row Purl 10A, 46B, 10A. (66sts).

shape mouth area

7th row Using A, (k3, m1) three times, k1, using B, k2, (m1, k3) fourteen times, m1, k2, using A, k1, (m1, k3) three times. (87sts)

8th-10th rows Stocking/stockinette stitch, 13A, 61B, 13A.

shape nose area, keeping 13A at each end.

11th row K39, skpo, k5, k2tog, k39.

12th row P38, p2tog, p5, p2togb, p38.

13th row K37, skpo, k5, k2tog, k37.

14th row P36, p2togb, p5, p2tog, p36.

15th row K26, (k2tog) twice, k5, skpo, k5, k2tog, k5, (skpo) twice, k26.

16th row Purl 13A, 47B, 13A.

17th row Knit 13A, using B (k1, k2tog) six times, k11, (skpo, k1) six times, 13A. (61sts)

18th row Purl 13A, 35B, 13A.

19th-36th rows eye section, follow chart. Break B and C.

37th-46th rows Using A, stocking/stockinette stitch.

shape head

47th row K3, (k2tog, k5) 8 times, k2tog.

48th row and alt rows P.

49th row K2, (k2tog, k4) 8 times, k2tog.

51st row K1, (k2tog, k3) 8 times, k2tog.

53rd row K2tog, (k2, k2tog) 8 times.

54th row (P2tog, p1) 8 times, p1.

55th row K1, (k2tog) 8 times.

Break yarn, leaving length for sewing. Thread yarn through remaining sts, pull together and fasten securely. Weave in any loose ends. RS together, join back seam, leaving cast on edge open.

legs (make 2)

Using A, cast on 6sts.

1st row (WS) and alt rows P.

2nd row (Inc) five times, k1.

4th row (Inc) ten times, k1.

6th row K2, m1, k7, m1, k3, m1, k7, m1, k2.

8th row K2, m1, k9, m1, k3, m1, k9, m1, k2. (29sts)

9th-15th rows Stocking/stockinette stitch.

Join in A. Working in stripes of 6 rows B, 6 rows A, continue in stocking/stockinette stitch until work measures approx. 38 cm (15 in), ending with a completed stripe.
Cast/bind off.

arms (make 2)

Using A, cast on 4sts.
1st row (WS) and alt rows P.
2nd row (Inc) 3 times, k1.
4th row (Inc) 6 times, k1.
6th row K2, m1, (k3, m1) 3 times, k2.
8th row (K2, m1) twice, (k3, m1) three times, k2, m1, k2. (23sts)
9th-15th rows Stocking/stockinette stitch.
Join in A. Working in stripes of 6 rows B, 6 rows A, continue until work measures approx. 30 cm (12 in), ending with a completed stripe.
Cast/bind off.

tail

Using A, cast on 4 sts.
1st row (WS) and alt rows P.
2nd row (Inc, k1) twice.
4th row (Inc, k1) 3 times.
6th row K1, (inc, k1) 4 times. 13sts
Continue in stocking/stockinette stitch until work measures 20 cm (8 in).
Cast/bind off.

ears (make 2)

Using B, cast on 14sts.
Work 8 rows in stocking/stockinette stitch.
9th row Skpo, k10, k2tog.
10th row P.
11th row Skpo, k8, k2tog.
12th row P2tog, p6, p2tog.
13th row Change to A, cast on 1st, knit.
14th row Cast on 2sts, purl.
15th row Cast on 1st, knit.
16th row P.
17th row Cast on 1st, knit.
18th row Cast on 1st, purl.
19th-24th rows Stocking/stockinette stitch.
Cast/bind off.

finishing

Weave in any loose ends.
Arms, legs and tail With RS together, sew long seam, leaving cast/bound off edge open. Turn RS out, stuff firmly and close opening
Body Stuff head and body firmly. Ensure that seam is centre back and close lower body opening.
Ears Fold in half, RS together, join side seams. Turn RS out, stuff lightly and close lower edge.
Mouth Embroider mouth using yarn A.
Cut eyes from felt and sew into place.
Attach arms, legs and ears and tail.

eyes

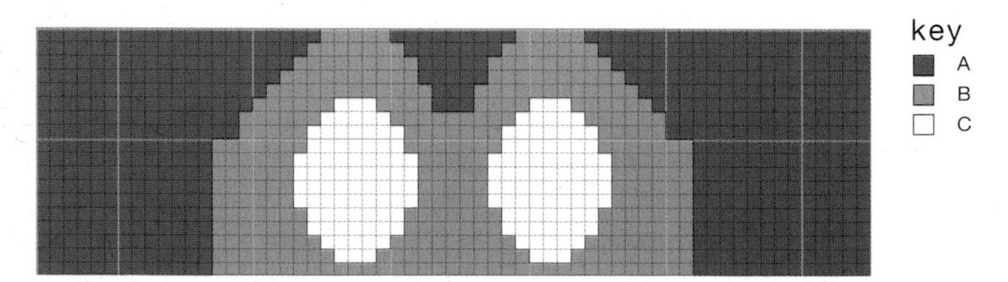

key
- A
- B
- C

floppy dog

This is an ideal doggie as he never needs to be taken out for a walk on cold days. He will sit patiently and make no noise as he waits for his bedtime cuddle.

size

Approx. 31 cm (12 in) tall

materials

2 50 g (1¾ oz) balls of Jaeger Baby Merino DK in main colour **M** (soft grey/Flannel 228) and 1 ball in **C** (pale brown/Choco 188)
Pair of 3.25 mm (US 3) knitting needles
Knitter's sewing needle
Washable stuffing
Embroidery needle
Pink velvet ribbon

tension/gauge

26 sts and 36 rows to 10 cm (4 in) square over stocking/stockinette stitch using 3.25 mm (US 3) needles.

abbreviations

See page 17.

charts

See page 140.

body and head

Start at lower edge

Using M, cast on 20sts.

1st row (WS) and alt rows P.

2nd row K4, m1, k2, m1, (k4, m1) twice, k2, m1, k4. (25sts)

4th row K1, m1, k4, m1, k2, m1, k5, m1, k1, m1, k5, m1, k2, m1, k4, m1, k1. (33sts)

6th row K.

8th row K7, m1, k2, m1, k15, m1, k2, m1, k7. (37sts)

10th row K.

12th row K2, m1, k6, m1, k2, m1, k7, m1, k3, m1, k7, m1, k2, m1, k6, m1, k2. (45sts)

13th-17th rows Stocking/stockinette stitch.

body patch

Using stocking/stockinette stitch and intarsia technique, work 1st–29th rows from body patch chart.

shape top of body

1st row (K3, k2tog) twice, k2, (skpo, k3) twice, k1, (k3, k2tog) twice, k2, (skpo, k3) twice. (37sts)

2nd-4th rows Stocking/stockinette stitch.

5th row (K2, k2tog) twice, k2, (skpo, k2) twice, k1, (k2, k2tog) twice, k2, (skpo, k2) twice. (29sts)

6th-8th rows Stocking/stockinette stitch.

shape head

1st row (K2, m1, k3, m1) twice, k3, m1, (k1, m1) three times, k3, (m1, k3, m1, k2) twice. (41sts)

2nd row P.

3rd row K18, m1, k2, m1, k1, m1, k2, m1, k18. (45sts)

4th-10th rows Stocking/stockinette stitch.

11th row K19, k2tog, k3, skpo, k19.

12th row P18, p2togb, p3, p2tog, p18.

13th row K17, k2tog, k3, skpo, k17.

14th row P.

15th row K16, k2tog, k3, skpo, k16. (37sts)

16th row P.

eye patch

Using stocking/stockinette stitch and intarsia technique, work 1st–10th rows from eye patch chart.

27th row K1, (k3, k2tog) 7 times, k1.

28th row P.

29th row K1, (k2, k2tog) 7 times, k1.

30th row P.

31st row K1, (k1, k2tog) 7 times, k1.

32nd row (P2tog) 8 times.

Break yarn, leaving a length for sewing. Thread yarn through remaining sts, pull together and secure firmly. With RS together, sew back seam leaving cast on edge open.

feet and legs

Start at foot.

Using M, cast on 30 sts.

1st row (Inc, k13, inc) twice.

2nd row P.

3rd row (Inc, k15, inc) twice. (38sts)

4th-8th rows Stocking/stockinette stitch.

9th row K15, (skpo) twice, (k2tog) twice, k15.

10th row P.

11th row K11, (skpo) three times, (k2tog) three times, k11.

12th row P.

13th row K8, (skpo) three times, (k2tog) three times, k8. (22sts)

14th-36th rows Stocking/stockinette stitch.

Cast/bind off.

Make second foot and leg to match.

arms (make 2)

Using M, cast on 8sts.

1st row (Inc, k1) 4 times.

2nd row P.

3rd row (K2, m1) twice, k4, (m1, k2) twice.

4th row P.

5th row (K3, m1) twice, k4, (m1, k3) twice. (20sts)

6th-30th rows Stocking/stockinette stitch.

31st and 32nd rows Cast/bind off 3sts, work to end.

33rd-35th rows Dec each end.

36th row P.

Cast/bind off.

Make second arm to match.

ears

Using M, cast on 8sts.

Work 48 rows in stocking/stockinette stitch, inc each end of 3rd and 7th rows, dec each end of 21st, 23rd and 24th rows, inc each end of 26th, 27th and 29th rows and dec each end of 43rd and 47th rows.

Cast/bind off. Make second ear to match.

tail

Using M, cast on 12sts.

Work 16 rows in stocking/stockinette stitch.

17th row K2tog, k3, (inc) twice, k3, k2tog.

18th row P.

19th-22nd rows Work as 17th–18th rows, twice. (12sts)

23rd row K2tog, knit to last 2sts, k2tog.

24th row P.

25th-30th rows Work as 23rd–24th rows, 3 times. (4sts)

31st row (K2tog) twice.

32nd row P2tog, fasten off.

finishing

Weave in any loose ends.

Legs With RS together, join leg and foot seam. Turn RS out and stuff lightly to give floppy effect, close cast/bound off edge.

Arms With RS together, join arm seam. Turn RS out and stuff lightly to give floppy effect.

Body Stuff lightly to give floppy effect and close lower edge, make sure that seam to head is at centre back. Attach legs to lower edge. Attach arms to body, adding stuffing if necessary.

Ears Fold ear in half, RS together and sew side seams. Turn RS out. Attach to head.

Tail With RS together sew seam. Turn RS out and stuff. Close opening and attach to back seam.

Embroider face, see photograph. Tie ribbon around neck and stitch in place if preferred.

body patch

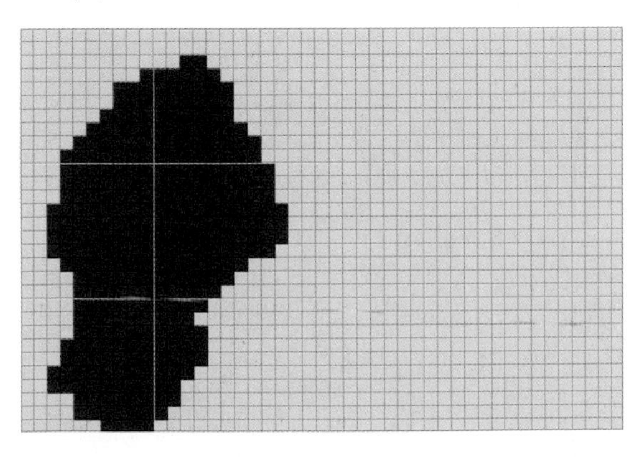

key

M

C

eye patch

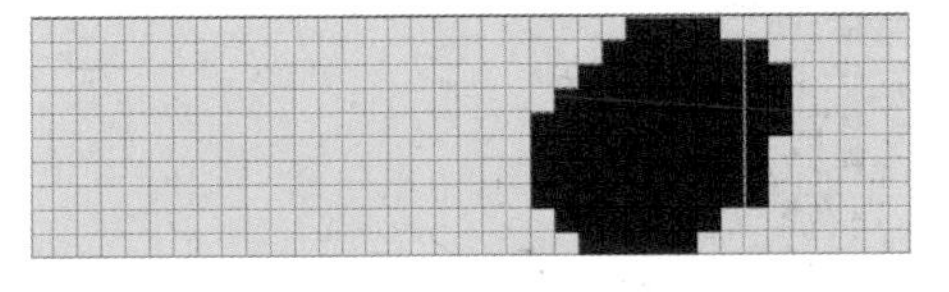

key

M

C

roaring dinosaur

This friendly dinosaur will have prime position in any little explorer's bedroom. Small boys will just love this toy as they seem to have an endless fascination with all that roars.

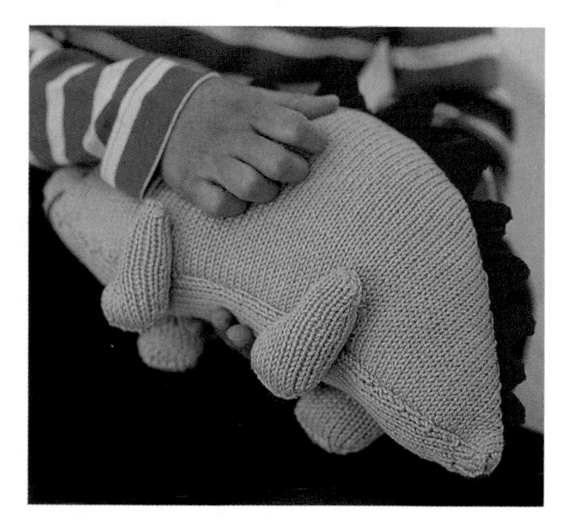

size

Approx. 25 cm (10 in) long

materials

2 50 g (1¾ oz) balls of Rowan Cotton Glace in main colour **M** (green/Shoot 814) and 1 ball in **C** (red/Poppy 741)
Pair of 3.25 mm (US 3) knitting needles
Knitter's sewing needle
Washable stuffing
Embroidery needle
Blue embroidery thread for face

tension/gauge

24 sts and 34 rows to 10 cm (4 in) square over stocking/stockinette stitch using 3.25 mm (US 3) needles.

abbreviations

See page 17.

first half of body

Using M, cast on 63sts.

1st row (RS) K.

2nd row (head end) Cast on 4sts, purl to end.

3rd and 4th rows Work as 1st and 2nd rows.

5th row (tail end) Cast/bind off 3sts, knit to end.

6th row Cast on 4sts, purl to end, place marker at end of row.

7th row K2tog, knit to end.

8th row Cast on 4sts, purl to end.

9th and 10th rows Work as 7th and 8th rows.

11th row K2tog, knit to end.

12th row Purl to last 2sts, p2tog.

13th row K.

14th row Purl to last 2sts, p2tog.

15th row K2tog, knit to end.

16th row P.

17th row K2tog, knit to end.

18th row Cast/bind off 5sts, purl to last 2sts, p2tog.

19th row K.

20th row Cast/bind off 5sts, purl to last 2sts, p2tog. (61sts)

21st row K2tog, knit to last 2sts, k2tog, place marker at end of row.

22nd row P.

23rd row K2tog, knit to last 2sts, k2tog.

24th row P2tog, purl to last 2sts, p2tog.

25th row K.

26th row P2tog, purl to last 2sts, p2tog.

27th row K2tog, knit to last 2sts, k2tog.

28th row P.

29th and 30th rows Work as 23rd and 24th rows. (47sts)

31st row K2tog, knit to end.

32nd row P2tog, purl to end.

33rd and 34th rows Work as 27th and 28th rows.

35th row K2tog, knit to last 2sts, k2tog.

36th row P2tog, purl to end.

37th and 38th rows Work as 31st and 32nd rows.

39th and 40th rows Work as 27th and 28th rows. (36sts)

41st-46th rows Cast/bind off 3sts, work to end.

Cast/bind off.

second half of body

Work as First Half of Body, but as a mirror image by reading purl for knit and knit for purl.

(eg: **1st row** P.

2nd row Cast on 4sts, knit to end.)

back legs (make 2)

Using M, cast on 17sts.

1st row Inc, k6, inc, k1, inc, k6, inc.

2nd row Inc, purl to last st, inc.

3rd row K11, m1, k1, m1, k11. (25sts)

4th-8th rows Stocking/stockinette stitch.

9th row K8, (k2tog) twice, k1, (skpo) twice, k8.

10th row P.

11th row K6, (k2tog) twice, k1, (skpo) twice, k6.

12th row P.

13th row K7, s1, k2tog, psso, k7. (15sts)

14th-22nd rows Stocking/stockinette stitch.

23rd row K2tog, k4, s1, k2tog, psso, k4, k2tog.

24th row P.

25th row K2tog, k2, s1, k2tog, psso, k2, k2tog.

26th row P.

Cast/bind off.

front legs (make 2)

Using M, cast on 13sts.

1st row Inc, k4, inc, k1, inc, k4, inc.

2nd row Inc, purl to last st, inc.

3rd row K9, m1, k1, m1, k9. (21sts)

4th-6th rows Stocking/stockinette stitch.

7th row K6, (k2tog) twice, k1, (skpo) twice, k6.

8th row P.

9th row K5, k2tog, s1, k2tog, psso, skpo, k5. (13sts)

10th-22nd rows Stocking/stockinette stitch.

23rd row K2tog, k3, s1, k2tog, psso, k3, k2tog.

24th row P.

25th row K2tog, k1, s1, k2tog, psso, k1, k2tog.

26th row P.

Cast/bind off.

gusset

Start at tail end.

Using M, cast on 3sts.

1st row K.

2nd row P.

3rd row Inc, k1, inc.

4th-8th rows Stocking/stockinette stitch.

9th row Inc at each end.

10th-27th rows Work as rows 4-9, 3 times. (13sts)

28th-86th rows Stocking/stockinette stitch.

87th row K2tog, knit to last 2sts, k2tog.

88th-92nd rows Stocking/stockinette stitch.

93rd-110th rows Work as rows 87-92, 3 times.

111th row K2tog, k1, k2tog.

112th row P.

Cast/bind off.

spines

Start at tail end.

Using C, cast on 1st.

1st row Inc.

2nd row Inc, k1.

3rd row K1, p1, inc.

4th row Inc, k1, p1, k1. (5sts)

5th row (K1, p1) twice, k1.

6th row P2tog, k1, p1, k1.

7th row K1, p1, k2tog.

8th row P2tog, k1.

9th row K2.

10th-17th rows Work as rows 2-9.

*Keeping moss st correct as now set, inc 1 st at shaped edge of next 5 rows. (7 sts)

Work 1 row.

Dec 1 st at shaped edge of next 5 rows. (2 sts)

Work 1 row.*

Rep last 12 rows twice more.

Inc 1 st at shaped edge of next 7 rows. (9 sts)

Work 1 row.

Dec 1 st at shaped edge of next 7 rows. (2 sts)

Work 1 row.

Rep last 16 rows 3 times more.

Rep from * to * once more.

Inc 1 st at shaped edge of next 3 rows. (5 sts)

Work 1 row.

Dec 1 st at shaped edge of next 3 rows. (2 sts)

Next row K2tog and fasten off.

finishing

Weave in any loose ends.

Body Pin and tack straight edge of spines to RS of a half body between markers. Place body pieces RS together and stitch from tail to nose, ensuring spines are included in stitching. Join straight seam at nose. Pin gusset to cast on edge from tail to nose. Stitch around gusset leaving an opening for stuffing. Turn RS out. Stuff firmly and close opening.

Legs RS facing, join leg seam, leaving cast on edge open. Turn RS out. Stuff firmly and attach legs to body. Embroider face, see photograph.

cute creations

slithery snake

Coil him up and slide him around the furniture; this stripy snake is an ideal playmate. His colourful stripes make a great way to use up odd balls of yarn.

size

Approx. 90 cm (35½ in) long

materials

2 50 g (1¾ oz) balls of Rowan Handknit Cotton DK in **A** (dark green/Slippery 316) and 1 ball in **B** (dark pink/Slick 313), **C** (red/Rosso 215), **D** (orange/Mango Fool 319), **E** (light green/Gooseberry 219), **F** (yellow/Buttercup 320), **G** (light pink/Sugar 303), **H** (mauve/Lupin 305), **J** (purple/Diana 287) and **K** (turquoise/Seafarer 318)
Pair of 3.25 mm (US 3) knitting needles
Knitter's sewing needle
Washable stuffing
Red felt for tongue
2 1½ cm (½ in) white buttons

tension/gauge

22sts and 30 rows to 10 cm (4 in) square over stocking/stockinette stitch using 3.25 mm (US 3) needles.

abbreviations

See page 17.

to make

Start at head

Using A, cast on 12sts.

1st row K.

2nd row P.

3rd row (K1, inc) twice, k3, inc, k1, inc, k2.

4th row P2, inc, p1, inc, p5, inc, p1, inc, p3.

5th row K.

6th row P3, inc, p1, inc, p7, inc, p1, inc, p4.

7th row K4, inc, k1, inc, k9, inc, k1, inc, k5.

8th row P.

9th row K5, inc, k1, inc, k11, inc, k1, inc, k6.

10th row P6, inc, p1, inc, p13, inc, p1, inc, p7.

11th row K.

12th row P7, inc, p1, inc, p15, inc, p1, inc, p8.

13th row K8, inc, k1, inc, k17, inc, k1, inc, k9.

14th row P.

15th row K9, inc, k1, inc, k19, inc, k1, inc, k10.

16th row P10, inc, p1, inc, p21, inc, p1, inc, p11. (52sts)

17th row K.

18th row P11, (inc) three times, p23, (inc) three times, p12. (58sts)

19th row K12, (inc) four times, k25, (inc) four times, k13. (66sts)

20th-30th rows Stocking/stockinette stitch

31st row K14, skpo, k1, k2tog, k28, skpo, k1, k2tog, k14.

32nd row P.

33rd row K13, skpo, k1, k2tog, k26, skpo, k1, k2tog, k13.

34th row P.

35th row K12, skpo, k1, k2tog, k24, skpo, k1, k2tog, k12. (54sts)

36th-38th rows Stocking/stockinette stitch.

39th row K6, k2tog, k11, skpo, k12, k2tog, k11, skpo, k6.

40th-44th rows Stocking/stockinette stitch.

45th row K5, k2tog, k11, skpo, k10, k2tog, k11, skpo, k5. (46sts)

46th row P.

Head section complete. Continue with body. Work 10-row stripe stocking/stockinette stitch sequence as follows: B, C, D, E, F, G, H, J, K, E, B, D, F, C, J. (196th row).

Start body shaping

1st-10th rows Using yarn K.

11th row G (K6, k2tog) 6 times, k6. (41sts)

12th-20th rows G.

21st-30th rows B.

31st row A (K5, k2tog) 5 times, k6. (36sts)

32nd-40th rows A.

41st-44th rows E.

45th row E (K4, k2tog) 6 times. (30sts)

46th-50th rows E.

51st-60th rows H.

61st row G (K3, k2tog) 6 times. (24sts)

62nd-70th rows G.

71st row J (K2, k2tog) 6 times. (18sts)

72nd-78th rows J

79th row J (K1, k2tog) 6 times. (12sts).

80th-84th rows J.

85th row J (K2tog) 6 times. (6sts).

86th-88th rows J

89th row J (K2tog) 3 times.

90th row P3tog, fasten off.

finishing

Weave in any loose ends.

With RS together, join belly seam leaving an opening for stuffing. Turn RS out, stuff firmly and close opening. Cut tongue from felt and attach. Sew on buttons for eyes.

butterfly

Happy flappy little wings will amuse and delight little ones. The cheerful colours and textured wings, lined with soft felt, make this toy great for little fingers to hold.

size

Approx. 15 cm (6 in) high and wide

materials

Small amounts of Rowan Handknit DK cotton in **A** (blue/Diana 287) and **B** (aqua/Seafarer 318) for body, **C** (red/Rosso 215) and **D** (pink/Slick 313) for lower wings, **G** (pale orange/Mango Fool 319) and **H** bright orange/Flame 254) for upper wings
Pair of 3.75 mm (US 5) knitting needles
Knitter's sewing needle
Small amount of washable stuffing
Felt for underside of wings and antennae
Embroidery needle
Embroidery threads, various colours.

tension/gauge

21 sts and 30 rows to 10 cm (4 in) square over stocking/stockinette stitch using 3.75 mm (US 5) needles.

abbreviations

See page 17.

charts

See page 140.

body

Using A, cast on 10sts.

1st row (K1, inc) five times. (15sts)

2nd-40th rows Stocking/stockinette stitch, starting with a purl row. Break A.

41st-51st rows Join in B, continue in stocking/stockinette stitch.

51st row (K2tog) seven times, k1. (8sts)

52nd row P.

53rd row (K2tog) four times, break yarn B leaving a length for sewing.

Thread yarn through remaining sts and secure firmly. With RS together, join head section. Join lower body section leaving cast on edge open for stuffing. Turn RS out stuff firmly. Close opening.

upper wings

right

Using H cast on 11sts.

Working in moss/seed stitch with stocking/stockinette stitch dot in G, follow chart A.

left

Using H cast on 11sts.

Working in moss/seed stitch with stocking/stockinette stitch dot in G, follow chart B.

lower wings

right

Using C cast on 9sts.

Working in moss/seed stitch with stocking/stockinette stitch dot in D, follow chart C.

left

Using C cast on 9sts.

Working in moss/seed stitch with stocking/stockinette stitch dot in D, follow chart D.

wings A/wings B/wings C/wings D

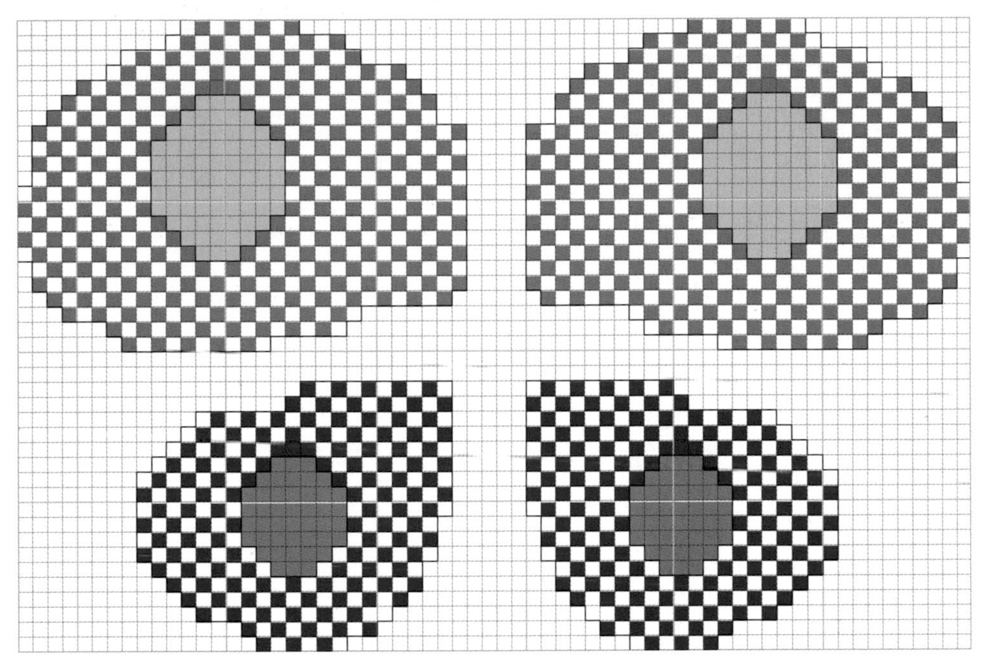

key

- C
- D
- G
- H

finishing

Weave in any loose ends. Press wing pieces using a warm iron over a damp cloth. Using wing pieces as a template, cut out shapes from felt material for back of wings and blanket stitch into place using embroidery thread. Join to body part, see chart. Cut out strips of felt for antennae and attach to head as in photograph. Embroider head details.

jumbo elephant

Always a favourite character, this special elephant has gorgeous blanket-stitched ears and a soft squishy trunk. He's sure to become a treasured friend for any little person.

size

Approx. 20 cm (8 in) tall

materials

2 50 g (1¾ oz) balls of Jaeger Baby Merino DK in pale blue/ Powder 222
Pair of 3.25 mm (US 3) knitting needles
Knitter's sewing needle
Washable stuffing
Blue felt for ears
Embroidery needle
Blue embroidery thread for ears
2 1 cm (⅜ in) buttons

tension/gauge

26 sts and 36 rows to 10 cm (4 in) square over stocking/stockinette stitch using 3.25 mm (US 3) needles.

abbreviations

See page 17.

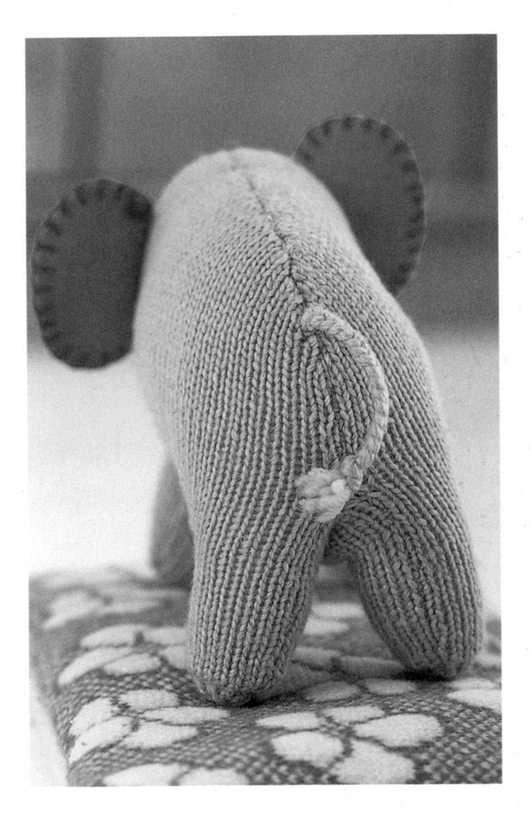

front leg

Cast on 11sts.

Work 22 rows in stocking/stockinette stitch, starting with a knit row. Leave sts on a spare needle.

back leg

Cast on 11sts.

Work 17 rows in stocking/stockinette stitch, starting with a knit row.

18th row Cast on 7sts, purl.

19th row K.

20th and 21st rows Work as rows 18 and 19.

22nd row Cast on 7sts, purl.

23rd row Knit across back leg, knit across front leg to last st, inc. (43sts)

24th-30th rows Stocking/stockinette stitch. Leave on spare needle. Do not break yarn.

trunk

Using second ball of yarn, cast on 6sts.

1st row K.

2nd row Cast on 2sts, purl.

3rd row Cast on 3sts, knit.

4th and 5th rows Work as rows 2 and 3.

6th row Inc, purl to end.

7th row Inc, knit to end. (18sts)

8th row P. Break yarn.

body

Return to legs.

31st row Knit across legs, knit across trunk to last st, inc. (62sts)

32nd row P.

33rd row Knit to last st, inc. (63sts)

34th row P.

35th row K52, cast/bind off 5sts, k5, inc.

Working on last 7sts

36th row P.

37th row K2tog, knit to end.

38th row P.

39th row K2tog, knit to last st, inc.

40th row P.

41st row K2tog, knit to end.

42nd row P2tog, p1, p2tog.

Cast/bind off.

WS facing, rejoin yarn to body.

36th row P. (52sts)

37th row Knit to last 2sts, k2tog.

38th and 39th rows Stocking/stockinette stitch.

40th row P2tog, purl to end.

41st and 42nd rows Stocking/stockinette stitch.

43rd-45th rows Work as rows 37-39.

46th row P2tog, purl to last 2sts, p2tog.

47th and 48th rows Stocking/stockinette stitch.

49th row Knit to last 2sts, k2tog.

50th row Purl to last 2sts, p2tog.
51st row K.
52nd row P2tog, purl to end.
53rd row K2tog, knit to end.
54th row P.
55th row K2tog, knit to last 2sts, k2tog.
56th row P.
57th row K2tog, knit to end.
58th row P2tog, purl to last 2sts, p2tog.
59th row K2tog, knit to end.
60th row P2tog, purl to last 2sts, p2tog. (35sts)
61st row Cast/bind off 5sts, knit to last 2sts, k2tog.
62nd row P2tog, purl to end.
63rd row Work as row 61.
64th row Cast/bind off 3sts, purl to end.
65th row Cast/bind off 7sts, knit to end.
66th row Cast/bind off 5sts, purl to end.
67th row Cast/bind off.
Make a second piece as a mirror image by reading knit for purl and purl for knit.
(Eg: Front leg
Cast on 11sts.
Work 22 rows in stocking/stockinette stitch starting with a purl row.)

gusset

Work 1st–27th rows of legs.
Cast/bind off.
Make second piece as a mirror image by reading knit for purl and purl for knit.
(Eg: Front leg – cast on 11sts
Work 32 rows in stocking/stockinette stitch starting with a purl row.)

feet (make 4)

Cast on 22sts.
1st row K.
2nd row (P2tog) 11 times.
3rd row (K2tog) 5 times, k1.
4th row (P2tog) 3 times. Break yarn leaving a length for sewing. Thread yarn through remaining stitches, pull tightly and secure, join small side seam to make a circle.

tail

Cut six 35 cm (14 in) lengths of yarn. Knot together at one end. Divide lengths into three 2-strand sections and plait. Finish with a knot. Trim tail end.

finishing

Weave in any loose ends.
Press pieces using a warm iron over a damp cloth.
With RS together, join cast/bound off edges of gusset. Join outside leg seams to main pieces. Pin a foot circle into place and stitch. Join inside leg seams. Repeat for other 3 legs. Join remainder of jumbo leaving opening at rear end for stuffing. Stuff firmly. Attach tail and close opening. Using ear template (see page 141), cut two ears facing each other, to make a left and right ear. Using embroidery thread blanket stitch around ears. Attach ears. Sew on buttons for eyes.

colourful mouse

Knit a whole host of these perky mice in a multitude of vibrant colours. They are quick and easy to knit and make a sweet toy to fit into any little child's pocket.

size

13 cm (5 in) long x 10 cm (4 in) high

materials

Small amounts of Jaeger Matchmaker Merino DK in 2 colours, **A** (light) and **B** (dark)
Pair of 3.25 mm (US 3) knitting needles
Knitter's sewing needle
Washable stuffing
Embroidery needle
Embroidery thread to complement yarn
Felt for ears to complement yarn

tension/gauge

24 sts and 34 rows to 10 cm (4 in) square over stocking/stockinette stitch using 3.25 mm (US 3) needles.

abbreviations

See page 17.

body

Using A, cast on 3sts.

1st row (WS) P.

2nd row (Inc) 3 times. (6sts)

3rd row P.

4th row (K2, m1) twice, k2.

5th row P.

6th row K2, m1, k4, m1, k2.

7th row P.

8th row (K2, m1) 4 times, k2. (14sts)

9th row P.

10th row K2, m1, k10, m1, k2.

11th row P.

12th row (K2, m1, k5, m1) twice, k2. (20sts)

13th row P.

14th row K2, m1, k16, m1, k2.

15th row Join in yarn B, purl.

16th row Inc, k9, m1, k2, m1, k9, inc. (26sts)

17th row Using A, purl.

18th row K. Inc each end.

19th row Using B, purl.

20th row K. (28sts)

21st-40th rows Repeat 17th–20th rows, 5 times. (38sts)

41st-43rd rows Work as 17th–19th rows. (40sts)

44th row K14, skpo, k1, skpo, k2, k2tog, k1, k2tog, k14.

45th row Using A, purl.

46th row K14, skpo, k4, k2tog, k14.

Cast/bind off.

under body

Using B, cast on 13sts.

Work 26 rows in stocking/stockinette stitch, dec each end of 9th, 17th and 24th rows.

27th-35th rows Change to A, continue in stocking/stockinette stitch. Dec each end of 28th and 35th rows.

36th row P.

37th row S1, k2tog, psso.

Fasten off.

back

Using B, cast on 13sts.

Work 16 rows in stocking/stockinette stitch, dec each end of 9th, 12th, 14th and 16th rows.

Cast/bind off.

tail

Cut four lengths of B and two lengths of A, each 18 cm (7 in). Knot together at one end. Make a plait, tying a knot at the end.

finishing

Weave in any loose ends.

Place body and underbody RS together, pin and stitch around base line. Insert back section and stitch around curved edge. Turn RS out and stuff firmly, inserting tail. Close last piece of baseline. Embroider eyes and nose. Cut out ears from felt and sew into place.

owl cushion

Have a hoot with this fabulous retro owl. His flappy felt wings finished with blanket-stitched edging give him that perfect homemade, nostalgic feeling.

size

30 cm (12 in) at widest point by 28 cm (11 in) high.

materials

1 50 g (1¾ oz) ball of Yarn Rowan Handknit Cotton DK in **A** (red/Rosso 215) and 2 balls in **B** (orange/Mango Fool 319)
Pair of 4 mm (US 6) knitting needles
Assorted shades of felt for eyes, beak and feathers and wings
Knitter's sewing needle
Washable stuffing

tension/gauge

20 sts and 28 rows to 10 cm (4 in) square over stocking/stockinette stitch using 4 mm (US 6) needles.

abbreviations

See page 17.

charts

See page 140.

front

Using A, cast on 16sts.
Working in stocking/stockinette stitch, follow chart, place markers for wings at *.

back

Using B throughout, cast on 16sts.
Working in stocking/stockinette stitch, follow front chart for shaping, place markers for wings at *.

finishing

Weave in any loose ends.
Cut felt pieces for eyes, beak and feathers and wings (blanket stitch if desired) from templates (see page 141). Sew to front of cushion.
With RS facing, sew around front and back of cushion, leaving cast on edges open. Turn RS out. Stuff cushion and close opening.

front

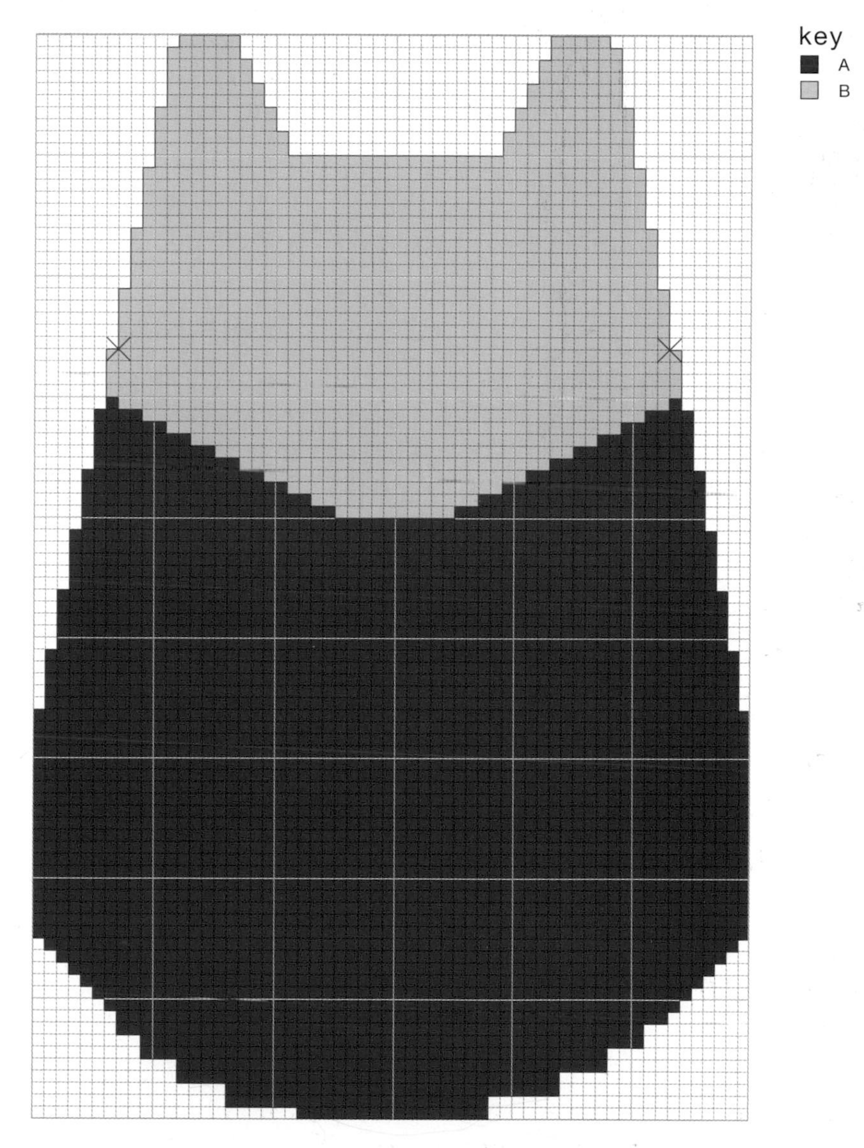

patchwork tortoise

The perfect project for using up oddments of yarn, this little tortoise will look sweet in any nursery. His button eyes add to the home-made effect.

size

Approx. 26 cm (10¼ in) from head to tail.

materials

1 50 g (1¾ oz) ball of Rowan Cotton Glace in main colour **M** (light turquoise/Pier 809) for body
Small amounts of Rowan Cotton Glace in green/Shoot 814, red/Poppy 741, yellow/Butter 795, pink/In the Pink 819, blue/Maritime 817 and lilac/Hyacinth 787 for shell
Pair of 3 mm (US 2/3) knitting needles
Knitter's sewing needle
Washable stuffing
Embroidery needle
2 1 cm (⅜ in) buttons

tension/gauge

26sts and 36 rows to 10 cm (4 in) square over stocking/stockinette stitch using 3 mm (US 2/3) needles.

abbreviations

See page 17.

under shell

Using M, cast on 12sts.

1st row K.

2nd row Cast on 3sts, purl.

3rd row Cast on 3sts, knit.

4th and 5th rows Work as rows 2 and 3. (24sts)

6th row Inc each end.

7th row K.

8th-17th rows Work rows 6 and 7, 5 times. (36sts)

18th row Inc each end.

19th and 20th rows Stocking/stockinette stitch.

21st row Inc each end. (40sts)

22nd-42nd rows Stocking/stockinette stitch.

43rd row Dec each end.

44th and 45th rows Stocking/stockinette stitch.

46th row Dec each end.

47th row K.

48th-57th rows Work as 46th and 47th rows, 5 times.

Row 58 Dec each end. (24sts)

59th-62nd rows Cast/bind off 3sts, work to end.

Cast/bind off.

legs (make 4)

Using M, cast on 6sts.

1st row (Inc, k1) 3 times.

2nd row P.

3rd row (K1, inc) 4 times, k1. (13sts)

4th-16th rows Stocking/stockinette stitch.

Cast/bind off.

head

Using M, cast on 6sts.

1st row (Inc, k1) 3 times.

2nd row P.

3rd row (K1, inc) 4 times, k1.

4th row P.

5th row (K1, inc) 6 times, k1. (19sts)

6th-8th rows Inc each end. (25sts)

9th-24th rows Stocking/stockinette stitch.

Cast/bind off.

tail

Using M, cast on 12sts.

1st-4th rows Stocking/stockinette stitch.

5th row K1, skpo, k2tog, k2, skpo, k2tog, k1.

6th-8th rows Stocking/stockinette stitch.

9th row (Skpo, k2tog) twice.

10th-12th rows Stocking/stockinette stitch.

13th row Skpo, k2tog.

14th row P2tog, fasten off.

shell edging

Using M, cast on 7sts.

1st row (K1, p1) twice, k3.

2nd row K3, (p1, k1) twice.

3rd–8th rows Work as 1st and 2nd rows, 3 times.

9th row (K1, p1) twice, turn.

10th row S1p, k1, p1, k1.

Repeat 1st–10th rows until the k3 edge fits around under shell.

Cast/bind off.

upper shell

Using any colour, cast on 6sts.

1st row Inc, knit to last st, inc.

2nd row P.

3rd–6th rows Work as rows 1 and 2, twice. (12sts)

7th row K.

8th row P2tog, purl to last 2sts, p2tog.

9th–12th rows Work as 7th and 8th rows, twice. (6sts)

Cast/bind off.

Make 21 more patches randomly in all colours (including M).

Sew 3 strips of 4 patches and 2 strips of 5 patches, joining cast on to cast/bound off edges.

Join strips.

fill in A (make 2)

Work 1st–6th rows of Upper Shell.

Cast/bind off.

fill in B (make 10)

Cast on 6sts.

1st row K.

2nd row P2tog, p2, p2tog.

3rd row K.

4th row (P2tog) twice.

5th row K2tog.

Fasten off.

Join fill in pieces.

finishing

Weave in any loose ends.

Body With RS facing, pin edging around under shell. With RS facing, pin upper shell at top, bottom and centre side to under edge. Ease excess material in each quarter and pin. Stitch around shell, ensuring edging is centre of 'sandwich' and leaving opening at tail end for stuffing. Turn RS out and stuff. Close opening.

Legs, head and tail RS facing, join side seams on. Turn RS out and stuff. Sew head and tail to the under shell, then sew on legs.

Sew on buttons for eyes.

dotty dog

With his dotted body and stripy tummy, he's a trendy pooch who will be at home in any room in your house. His floppy ears and comical face make him everyone's best friend.

size

Approx. 60 cm (24 in) long

materials

3 50 g (1¾ oz) balls of Yarn Rowan Handknit DK Cotton in main colour **M** (pale blue/Ice Water 239) and 1 ball in **A** (pink/Slick 313), **B** (red/Rosso 215), **C** (orange/Flame 254), **D** (light green/Gooseberry 219) and **E** (purple/Diana 287)
Pair of 3.25 mm (US 3) knitting needles
Knitter's sewing needle
Washable stuffing
Embroidery needle
Assorted shades of felt for eyes and ears.

tension/gauge

24 sts and 32 rows to 10 cm (4 in) square over stocking/stockinette stitch using 3.25 mm (US 3) needles.

abbreviations

See page 17.

upper body

Start at tail.

Using M, cast on 3sts.

1st row Inc, k1, inc.

2nd row P.

3rd row (Inc, k1) twice, inc.

4th row P.

5th row Inc, k3, m1, k3, inc. (11sts)

6th-18th rows Stocking/stockinette stitch.

shape body

19th-20th rows Cast on 10sts, work to end. Place marker at end of each row. (31sts)

21st-22nd rows Cast on 2sts, work to end.

23rd-25th rows Inc each end.

26th row P.

27th row Inc each end.

28th row Purl 13M, 2A, 28M.

29th row Inc, k26M, 4A, 11M, inc. (45sts)

30th row Purl 13M, 4A, 28M.

31st row Knit 28M, 4A, 13M.

32nd row Purl 14M, 2A, 29M.

These last 5 rows form 'dot' (i.e. 1st row 2sts, 2nd-4th rows 4sts, 5th row 2sts).

33rd-110th rows Stocking/stockinette stitch, placing 'dots' randomly on body.

shape head

Keep working 'dots' if desired, but no more 'dots' after 120th row.

111th-113th rows Dec each end.

114th row P.

115th row Dec each end.

116th-117th rows Work as 114th–115th rows. (35sts)

118th-120th rows Stocking/stockinette stitch.

121st row K15, k2tog, k1, skpo, k15.

122nd row P.

123rd row Dec each end.

124th row P.

125th row K13, k2tog, k1, skpo, k13.

126th-128th rows Stocking/stockinette stitch.

129th row K6, k2tog, k2, (k2tog) twice, k1, (skpo) twice, k2, skpo, k6. (23sts)

130th-132nd rows Stocking/stockinette stitch.

133rd row K2tog, k7, k2tog, k1, skpo, k7, k2tog.

134th-136th rows Stocking/stockinette stitch.

137th row K7, k2tog, k1, skpo, k7.

138th-140th rows Stocking/stockinette stitch.

141st row K2tog, k4, k2tog, k1, skpo, k4, k2tog.

142nd-144th rows Stocking/stockinette stitch.
145th row K4, k2tog, k1, skpo, k4.
146th row P.
Cast/bind off.

back legs (make 2)

Using M, cast on 17sts.
1st row Inc, k6, inc, k1, inc, k6, inc.
2nd row Inc, purl to last st, inc. (23sts)
3rd row K11, m1, k1, m1, k11. (25sts)
4th-8th rows Stocking/stockinette stitch.
9th row K8, (k2tog) twice, k1, (skpo) twice, k8.
10th row P.
11th row K6, (k2tog) twice, k1, (skpo) twice, k6.
12th row P.
13th row K7, s1, k2tog, psso, k7*. (15sts)
14th-26th rows Stocking/stockinette stitch.
27th row K2tog, k4, s1, k2tog, psso, k4, k2tog.
28th-30th rows Stocking/stockinette stitch.
31st row K2tog, k2, s1, k2tog, psso, k2, k2tog.
32nd row P.
Cast/bind off.

front legs (make 2)

Work as for back legs to *.
14th-22nd rows Stocking/stockinette stitch.
23rd row K2tog, k4, s1, k2tog, psso, k4, k2tog.
24th row P.
25th row K2tog, k2, s1, k2tog, psso, k2, k2tog.
26th row P.
Cast/bind off.

gusset

Work in stocking/stockinette stitch in 4-row stripes using the 'dot' colours randomly. Cast on 3sts.
1st-4th rows Stocking/stockinette stitch.
5th row Change colour, inc, knit to last st, inc.
6th-8th rows Stocking/stockinette stitch.
9th-20th rows Work 5th-8th rows, 3 times. (11sts)

21st-108th rows Work in stocking/stockinette stitch stripes.
109th-111th rows Change colour, stocking/stockinette stitch.
112th row P2tog, purl to last 2sts, p2tog.
113th-124th rows Work 109th-112th rows, 3 times. (3sts)
125th-128th rows Change colour, stocking/stockinette stitch.
Cast/bind off.

finishing

Weave in any loose ends.
Legs with RS facing, join leg seam, leaving cast on edge open. Turn RS out and stuff firmly.
Body with RS facing, join tail and back to markers on upper body. Pin gusset to remaining open edge of body. Stitch, leaving an opening for stuffing. Turn RS out and stuff. Close opening. Embroider nose as in photograph. Cut out eyes from felt and stitch in place. Cut two ears from template (see page 141). Attach ears to top of head. Attach legs to body.

stripy ball

Roll it, catch it...throw it! Every toddler needs a ball, and this gorgeously soft and colourful one is a brilliant early toy. It is sure to become a playtime favourite.

size

15 cm (6 in) in circumference

materials

Small amounts of Jaeger Baby Merino DK in **A** (Red 231), **B** (blue/Blue Ball 189), **C** (yellow/Gold 225), **D** (cream/Pearl 203), **E** (Orange 234) and **F** (green/Khaki 230)
Small amount of Jaeger Matchmaker Merino DK in **G** (violet/Azalea 897)
Pair of 3.75 mm (US 5) knitting needles
Knitter's sewing needle
Washable stuffing

tension/gauge

24 sts and 34 rows to 10 cm (4 in) square over stocking/stockinette stitch using 3.75 mm (US 5) needles.

abbreviations

See page 17.

charts

See page 140.

to make

The ball is made up in 6 sections, 3 plain and 3 striped.

plain sections

Using A, cast on 2sts.

Working in stocking/stockinette stitch, follow chart.

Repeat using B and C for sections 5 and 3.

striped sections

Work as for plain sections, but in 4-row stripes of D and E (section 2), D and F (section 4) and D and G (section 6).

finishing

Weave in any loose ends. Press pieces lightly using a warm iron over a damp cloth. With RS facing, join sections 1–6 together (alternating stripe and plain sections), leaving an opening for stuffing. Turn RS out. Stuff ball and close opening.

plain section

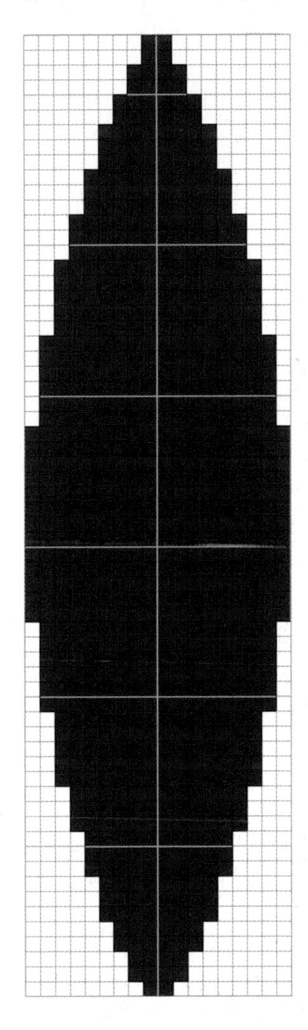

fish on the line

These colourful, jolly little fish make lovely decorations for a playroom or nursery window. A great toy to make in an evening and original idea for a child's room.

size

Approx. 10 cm (8 in) long

materials

1 50 g (¾ oz) ball of Jaeger Aqua Cotton DK in orange/Marigold 331, green/Herb 303, aqua/Tide 313, pink/India 322, red/Ruby 316 and yellow/Daffodil 330
Pair of 3.75 mm (US 5) knitting needles
Knitter's sewing needle
Washable stuffing
Wooden beads
Embroidery needle
Assorted embroidery threads
Blue cotton for stringing beads

tension/gauge

24 sts and 32 rows to 10 cm (4 in) square over stocking/stockinette stitch using 3.75 mm (US 5) needles.

abbreviations

See page 17.

to make

Make a fish in each colour.

side 1

Cast on 2sts.

Work from chart, reading odd rows right to left and even rows left to right.

Start with 1st row as a knit row.

side 2

Work a mirror image of side 1 by working from chart, reading odd rows right to left and even rows left to right, but start with 1st row as a purl row.

finishing

Weave in any loose ends.

Press pieces using a warm iron over a damp cloth. With RS together, sew around fish leaving tail edge open. Turn RS out and stuff tightly. Close opening. Embroider knot eyes to finish each fish. Using cotton, thread beads onto cotton to separate each fish, tying securely attached. Repeat this for each fish, ensuring beads are secure – so that they cannot be swallowed by a baby. Alternatively you could do small plaits in between each fish, if you do not want to use beads.

side 1/side 2

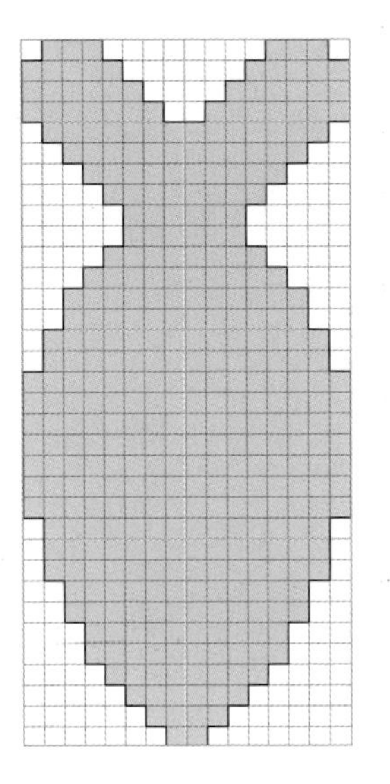

snappy crocodile

Keep this croc on your child's bed as he's a perfect size to snuggle up to. He'll protect them from monsters and make sure that the bed bugs won't bite.

size

Approx. 45 cm (18 in) long

materials

2 50 g (1¾ oz) balls of Yarn Rowan Wool Cotton in main colour **M** (green/Laurel 960)
Small amount of Jaeger Matchmaker Merino DK in **A** (cherry 656) for mouth, **B** (white 661) and **C** (black 681) for eyes
Pair of 3.25 mm (US 3) knitting needles
Felt for teeth and eyes
Knitter's sewing needle
Washable stuffing

tension/gauge

24 sts and 36 rows to 10 cm (4 in) square over stocking/stockinette stitch using 3.25 mm (US 3) needles.

abbreviations

See page 17.

top body

Start with upper body.

Using M, cast on 11sts.

Work 2 rows in stocking/stockinette stitch.

3rd row K1, inc, k6, inc, k2.

4th-6th rows Stocking/stockinette stitch.

7th row K1, inc, k8, inc, k2.

8th-10th rows Stocking/stockinette stitch.

11th row K1, inc, k10, inc, k2.

12th-14th rows Stocking/stockinette stitch.

15th row K1, inc, k12, inc, k2.

16th-18th rows Stocking/stockinette stitch.

19th row K1, inc, k14, inc, k2. (21sts)

20th-22nd rows Stocking/stockinette stitch, placing markers at each end of last row.

23rd row K2, inc, k14, inc, k3.

24th-26th rows Stocking/stockinette stitch.

27th row K3, inc, k14, inc, k4. (25sts)

28th-30th rows Stocking/stockinette stitch.

make eye ridges.

31st row K4, inc, k1, *k1, p1, k1, all into next st*, k11, work from * to * again, inc, k5. (31sts)

32nd row P.

33rd row K8, m1, k1, m1, k13, m1, k1, m1, k8. (35sts)

34th-50th rows Stocking/stockinette stitch.

start spine bumps

51st row K16, (inc) twice, k17.

52nd row P17, (inc) twice, p18.

53rd row K18, (inc) twice, k19. (41sts)

54th row P.

55th row K17, skpo, k3, k2tog, k17.

56th row P17, p2togb, p1, p2tog, p17.

57th row K17, s1, k2tog, psso, k17. (35sts)

58th-64th rows Stocking/stockinette stitch.

65th-120th rows Work as 51st-64th rows, 4 times.

121st row K5, k2tog, k9, (inc) twice, k10, skpo, k5.

122nd row P16, (inc) twice, p17.

123rd row K17, (inc) twice, k18.

124th row P.

125th row K16, skpo, k3, k2tog, k16.

126th row P16, p2tog, p1, p2togb, p16.

127th row K2tog, k3, k2tog, k9, s1, k2tog, psso, k9, skpo, k3, k2tog. (29sts)

128th-132nd rows Stocking/stockinette stitch.

133rd row K4, k2tog, k17, skpo, k4.

134th row P.

135th row K12, (inc) twice, k13.

136th row P13, (inc) twice, p14.

137th row K.

138th row P13, p2tog, p1, p2togb, p13.

139th row K2tog, k2, k2tog, k7, s1, k2tog, psso, k7, skpo, k2, k2tog. (23sts)

140th-144th rows Stocking/stockinette stitch.

145th row K3, k2tog, k5, (inc) twice, k6, skpo, k3.

146th row P10, (inc) twice, p11.

147th row K.

148th row P10, p2tog, p1, p2togb, p10.
149th row K2tog, k1, k2tog, k5, s1, k2tog, psso, k5, skpo, k1, k2tog. (17sts)
150th-152nd rows Stocking/stockinette stitch.
153rd row K2, k2tog, k9, skpo, k2.
154th-156th rows Stocking/stockinette stitch.
157th row (K2tog) twice, k7, (skpo) twice.
158th-160th rows Stocking/stockinette stitch.
161st row K1, (k2tog) twice, k1, (skpo) twice, k1. (7sts)
162nd row P.
163rd row K2, s1, k2tog, psso, k2.
164th row P.
165th row K2tog, k1, k2tog.
166th row P3tog.
Fasten off.

under body

Using M, cast on 11sts.
Work 1st-30th rows as Upper Body. (25sts)
31st-120th rows Stocking/stockinette stitch.
121st-165th rows Dec each end of 121st, 127th, 133rd, 139th, 145th, 149th, 153rd, 157th, 161st, 163rd and 165th rows .
166th row P3tog.
Fasten off.

feet (make 4)

Using M, cast on 13sts.
1st row Inc, k4, inc, k1, inc, k4, inc.
2nd row Inc, purl to last st, inc. (19sts)
3rd-6th rows Stocking/stockinette stitch.
7th row K7, skpo, k1, k2tog, k7.
8th row P6, p2tog, p1, p2togb, p6. (15sts)
9th-14th rows Stocking/stockinette stitch.
15th row K2tog, k4, s1, k2tog, psso, k4, k2tog.
16th row P.
17th row K2tog, k2, s1, k2tog, psso, k2, k2tog.
18th row P.
Cast/bind off.

mouth

Using red, cast on 9sts and work 42 rows in stocking/stockinette stitch, inc each end of 3rd, 7th, 11th,15th and 19th rows and dec each end of 25th, 29th, 33rd, 37th and 41st rows. Cast/bind off.

teeth

Cut strip of felt the length of mouth opening for upper and lower jaws. Cut zigzags from one edge of felt to make teeth shapes. Sew into place using white thread as you sew mouth together.

finishing

Weave in any loose ends.
Body with RS facing, join upper and under body from marker to marker leaving mouth open.
Stuff animal before finishing crocodile's teeth.
Legs with RS facing, join side seam, leaving cast/bound off edge open for stuffing. Turn RS out, stuff and attach to body, see photograph.
Cut out eyes from felt and sew in place.

charts

Charts are a really useful way of showing a pattern that has colour changes and shaping, but you need to know how to read them.

On the chart, each individual square represents one stitch, and each row of squares represents a row of knitting. The chart can show you what to do in a variety of ways. On this fish chart, the coloured area is the area to be knitted, and the empty squares help you see how the knitting is shaped. On some charts, the whole of the chart will be knitted, and the coloured areas will be sections knitted in a different colour. And, sometimes, a chart will combine both these styles. Unless otherwise stated, the charts are worked in stocking / stockinette stitch, RS knit, WS purl.

Where more than one stitch is decreased (or increased), you need to cast/bind off (or on) these stitches so the work is not distorted. And at the very end of the shape, the final stitches need to be cast/bound off once the last charted row has been worked – for this fish, you will cast / bind off the last 3 stitches.

Where a shape splits into two – like the tail of this fish – you need to work each section separately. Start by working the first row of stitches up to the point where the pattern splits. Slip all the stitches beyond this point onto a holder, turn the work and complete the first section, shaping as required.

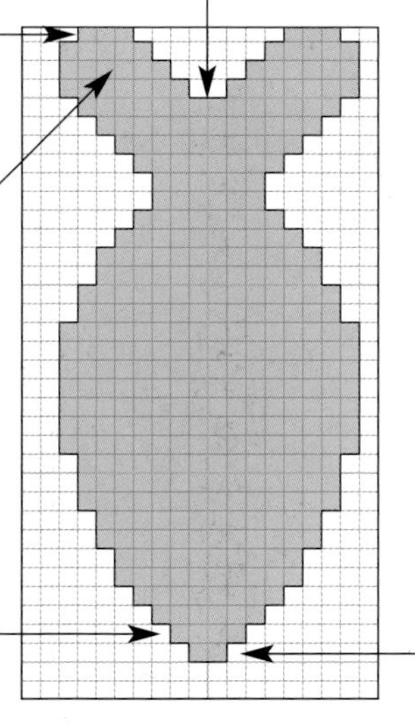

When the first section is complete, slip the stitches on the holder back onto the needles. Rejoin the yarn to the first stitch after the first section. Sometimes, as here, you will need to 'lose' some stitches between the sections. Do this by casting / binding off the required number of stitches at the beginning of the next row.

Start to follow the chart at its lowest edge. Here you will have been instructed in the pattern to cast on 2 stitches. The chart shows you should work the two stitches – indicated by the 2 coloured squares at the base of the fish shape. Usually the first row of a chart is a right side (RS) row and you will follow the chart by reading across the squares of one row from right to left. The next row will be a wrong side (WS) row and, for this row, read the chart from left to right. On the following row, read the chart from right to left again, then on the next row from left to right again, and so on.

Where the outline is shaped, stitches need to be increased or decreased. If the chart is one square wider on the next row, you need to increase a stitch at that edge. If it is narrower, you need to decrease a stitch.

templates

The templates here are at 50% of their actual size so you'll need to photocopy them at 200%.

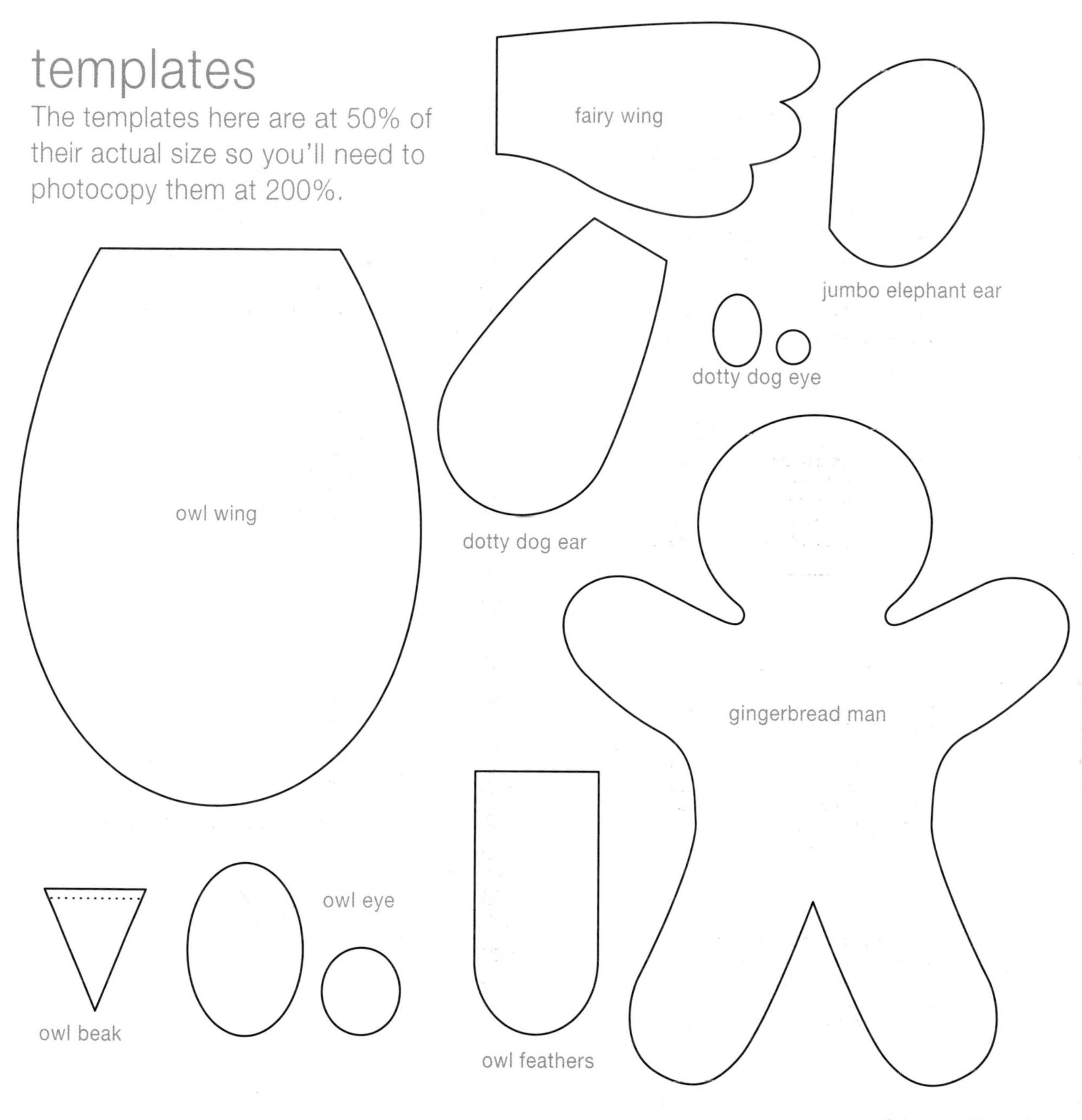

index

acknowledgements

author acknowledgements

Thank you to Adrian and Rozelle for the lovely styling and photographs. Thank you to Kitty and all the other models and to Eva for being such an expert knitter. Thanks too to Katy for asking me to write the book and for being so enthusiastic.

publisher acknowledgements

The Publishers would like to thank Ellie-May Bowden, Rachel Davies, Karla Dicker, Izzi Humphrey, Archie Miller, Abigail Obahor, Bibiana Obahor, Holly Painter, Anish Shah, Jessica Underhill, Jack Wescott, Kitty Wynne-Mellor and Connor Young for being such wonderful models.

Special photography
© Octopus Publishing Group Limited/Adrian Pope

Executive Editor Katy Denny
Editor Emma Pattison
Executive Art Editor Karen Sawyer
Designers Maggie Town and Beverly Price @ 126
Photographer Adrian Pope
Photography Styling & Art Direction Rozelle Betheim
Illustrator Kuo Kang Chen
Pattern Checker Stella Smith
Senior Production Controller Martin Croshaw